Perl Testing

A Developer's Notebook™

Other resources from O'Reilly

Related titles   Advanced Perl Programming   Perl Cookbook
Learning Perl   Perl in a Nutshell
Mastering Perl/Tk   Perl Template Toolkit
Perl 6 and Parrot Essentials   Practical mod_perl
Perl Best Practices   Programming Perl

oreilly.com   *dotnet.oreilly.com* is more than a complete catalog of O'Reilly books. You'll also find links to news, events, articles, weblogs, sample chapters, and code examples.

oreillynet.com is the essential portal for developers interested in open and emerging technologies, including new platforms, programming languages, and operating systems.

Conferences   O'Reilly brings diverse innovators together to nurture the ideas that spark revolutionary industries. We specialize in documenting the latest tools and systems, translating the innovator's knowledge into useful skills for those in the trenches. Visit *conferences.oreilly.com* for our upcoming events.

Safari Bookshelf (*safari.oreilly.com*) is the premier online reference library for programmers and IT professionals. Conduct searches across more than 1,000 books. Subscribers can zero in on answers to time-critical questions in a matter of seconds. Read the books on your Bookshelf from cover to cover or simply flip to the page you need. Try it today for free.

Perl Testing

A Developer's Notebook™

Ian Langworth and chromatic

O'REILLY®

Beijing · Cambridge · Farnham · Köln · Paris · Sebastopol · Taipei · Tokyo

Perl Testing: A Developer's Notebook™
by Ian Langworth and chromatic

Published by O'Reilly Media, Inc., 1005 Gravenstein Highway North, Sebastopol, CA 95472.

O'Reilly books may be purchased for educational, business, or sales promotional use. Online editions are also available for most titles (*safari.oreilly.com*). For more information, contact our corporate/institutional sales department: (800) 998-9938 or *corporate@oreilly.com*.

Editors:	Allison Randal
	Tatiana Apandi
Production Editor:	Adam Witwer
Cover Designer:	Edie Freedman
Interior Designer:	David Futato

Printing History:

July 2005:	First Edition.

 This book uses RepKover™, a durable and flexible lay-flat binding.

ISBN: 0-596-10092-2

[M]

Contents

The Developer's Notebook Series

So, you've managed to pick this book up. Cool. Really, I'm excited about that! Of course, you may be wondering why these books have the odd-looking, college notebook sort of cover. I mean, this is O'Reilly, right? Where are the animals? And, really, do you *need* another series? Couldn't this just be a cookbook? How about a nutshell, or one of those cool hacks books that seem to be everywhere? The short answer is that a developer's notebook is none of those things—in fact, it's such an important idea that we came up with an entirely new look and feel, complete with cover, fonts, and even some notes in the margin. This is all a result of trying to get something into your hands you can actually use.

It's my strong belief that while the nineties were characterized by everyone wanting to learn everything (Why not? We all had six-figure incomes from dot-com companies), the new millennium is about information pain. People don't have time (or the income) to read through 600-page books, often learning 200 things, of which only about 4 apply to their current job. It would be much nicer to just sit near one of the uber-coders and look over his shoulder, wouldn't it? To ask the guys that are neck-deep in this stuff why they chose a particular method, how they performed this one tricky task, or how they avoided that threading issue when working with piped streams. The thinking has always been that books can't serve that particular need—they can inform, and let you decide, but ultimately a coder's mind was something that couldn't really be captured on a piece of paper.

This series says that assumption is patently wrong—and we aim to prove it.

A Developer's Notebook is just what it claims to be: the often-frantic scribbling and notes that a true-blue alpha geek mentally makes when working with a new language, API, or project. It's the no-nonsense code that solves problems, stripped of page-filling commentary that often serves more as a paperweight than an epiphany. It's hackery, focused not on what is nifty or might be fun to do when you've got some free time (when's the last time that happened?), but on what you need to simply "make it work." This isn't a lecture, folks—it's a lab. If you want a lot of concept, architecture, and UML diagrams, I'll happily and proudly point you to our animal and nutshell books. If you want every answer to every problem under the sun, our omnibus cookbooks are killer. And if you are into arcane and often quirky uses of technology, hacks books simply rock. But if you're a coder, down to your core, and you just want to get on with it, then you want a Developer's Notebook. Coffee stains and all, this is from the mind of a developer to yours, barely even cleaned up enough for print. I hope you enjoy it...we sure had a good time writing them.

Notebooks Are...

Example-driven guides
> As you'll see in the "Organization" section, developer's notebooks are built entirely around example code. You'll see code on nearly every page, and it's code that *does something*—not trivial "Hello World!" programs that aren't worth more than the paper they're printed on.

Aimed at developers
> Ever read a book that seems to be aimed at pointy-haired bosses, filled with buzzwords, and feels more like a marketing manifesto than a programming text? We have too—and these books are the antithesis of that. In fact, a good notebook is incomprehensible to someone who can't program (don't say we didn't warn you!), and that's just the way it's supposed to be. But for developers...it's as good as it gets.

Actually enjoyable to work through
> Do you really have time to sit around reading something that isn't any fun? If you do, then maybe you're into thousand-page language references—but if you're like the rest of us, notebooks are a much better fit. Practical code samples, terse dialogue centered around practical examples, and even some humor here and there—these are the ingredients of a good developer's notebook.

About doing, not talking about doing

If you want to read a book late at night without a computer nearby, these books might not be that useful. The intent is that you're coding as you go along, knee deep in bytecode. For that reason, notebooks talk code, code, code. Fire up your editor before digging in.

Notebooks Aren't...

Lectures

We don't let just anyone write a developer's notebook—you've got to be a bona fide programmer, and preferably one who stays up a little too late coding. While full-time writers, academics, and theorists are great in some areas, these books are about programming in the trenches, and are filled with instruction, not lecture.

Filled with conceptual drawings and class hierarchies

This isn't a nutshell (there, we said it). You won't find 100-page indices with every method listed, and you won't see full-page UML diagrams with methods, inheritance trees, and flow charts. What you will find is page after page of source code. Are you starting to sense a recurring theme?

Long on explanation, light on application

It seems that many programming books these days have three, four, or more chapters before you even see any working code. I'm not sure who has authors convinced that it's good to keep a reader waiting this long, but it's not anybody working on *this* series. We believe that if you're not coding within 10 pages, something's wrong. These books are also chock-full of practical application, taking you from an example in a book to pulling things to work on your job, as quickly as possible.

Organization

Developer's Notebooks try to communicate different information than most books, and as a result, are organized differently. They do indeed have chapters, but that's about as far as the similarity between a notebook and a traditional programming book goes. First, you'll find that all the headings in each chapter are organized around a specific task. You'll note that we said *task*, not *concept*. That's one of the important things to get about these books—they are first and foremost about doing something. Each of these headings represents a single *lab*. A lab is just what it sounds like—steps to accomplish a specific goal. In fact, that's the first heading you'll see under each lab: "How do I do that?" This is the central question of each lab, and you'll find lots of down-and-dirty code and detail in these sections.

Some labs have some things not to do (ever played around with potassium in high school chemistry?), helping you avoid common pitfalls. Some labs give you a good reason for caring about the topic in the first place; we call this the "Why do I care?" section, for obvious reasons. For those times when code samples don't clearly communicate what's going on, you'll find a "What just happened" section. It's in these sections that you'll find concepts and theory—but even then, they are tightly focused on the task at hand, not explanation for the sake of page count. Finally, many labs offer alternatives, and address common questions about different approaches to similar problems. These are the "What about..." sections, which will help give each task some context within the programming big picture.

And one last thing—on many pages, you'll find notes scrawled in the margins of the page. These aren't for decoration; they contain tips, tricks, insights from the developers of a product, and sometimes even a little humor, just to keep you going. These notes represent part of the overall communication flow—getting you as close to reading the mind of the developer-author as we can. Hopefully they'll get you that much closer to feeling like you are indeed learning from a master.

And most of all, remember—these books are...

All Lab, No Lecture

—Brett McLaughlin, Series Creator

Preface

Is there any sexier topic in software development than software testing, at least besides game programming, 3D graphics, audio, high-performance clustering, cool web sites, and so on?

Okay, so software testing is low on the list. That's unfortunate, because good software testing can increase your productivity, improve your designs, raise your quality, ease your maintenance burdens, and help to satisfy your customers, coworkers, and managers. It's no surprise that the agile development techniques place such an emphasis on automated software testing—when it clicks for you and you understand it, you'll wonder how you ever wrote software without it.

Perl has a bit of a reputation for being hackish and unserious. It's certainly good for doing quick and dirty jobs quickly and dirtily. However, if you approach it with discipline, you'll find that it's suitable for big, serious projects. You probably already know this. You may not know how to apply the discipline, though. That's where this book can help.

Perl has a strong history of automated tests. The earliest release of Perl 1.0 the authors know of included a comprehensive test suite. It's only improved from there. The CPAN, a huge archive of freely available and reusable Perl code, exerts strong social pressure on contributors to write and maintain good test suites for their code. It also includes dozens of useful testing modules to make testing possible, or even easy.

Of course, your main job probably isn't all Perl all the time. It may be just one of a handful of good tools you use. That's fine. Learning how Perl's test tools work and how to put them together to solve all sorts of previously intractable problems can make you a better programmer in general. Besides, it's easy to use the Perl tools described here (and others that the future will bring) to handle all sorts of testing problems you encounter, even in other languages.

You don't have to be a die-hard free and open source software developer who lives, breathes, and dreams Perl to use this book. You just have to want to do your job a little bit better.

What This Book Covers

The nine chapters of this book cover testing in Perl, starting as if you've never written a test before and ending by exploring some of the testing problems you'll encounter in the real world. The authors expect you to know Perl already well enough to install and use Perl modules effectively in your own programs. You should have a decent understanding of Perl data structures and object-oriented programming. You need to have Perl newer than 5.6.0 installed, but the authors recommend at least Perl 5.6.1 and suggest that you consider upgrading to the latest version of the stable 5.8 series.

As for the chapters themselves, they discuss:

Writing basic tests
> This chapter explains everything you need to start writing and running tests, including how to install testing modules, how to understand test results, and the basic test functions you'll use in every test.

Improving your tests
> This chapter builds on the previous chapter, demonstrating further test techniques and modules. Once you're familiar with writing tests, you'll encounter some common tasks and troubles. Here's how to solve them.

Organizing and running tests well
> This chapter shows how to take advantage of the basic testing tools to customize them for your environment and projects. In particular, it shows how to write your own testing libraries and harnesses.

Bundling tests and code into projects
> Tests are just code, and all of the normal rules of disciplined coding apply. This chapter covers some of the issues you'll face when you want to distribute your project, especially the issues of non-code portions of your project.

Testing hard-to-test code
> Unit testing seems easy in theory, but complex projects have complex interactions that might seem impossibly untestable at first. This

chapter claims otherwise. It recommends another way of thinking that allows you to substitute testable code—under your control—for code that otherwise looks untestable.

Testing databases and their data

Many programs interact with databases: relational, object, and flat file. While these normally seem outside the purview of what you can test from Perl, there are simple and effective techniques to verifying that your code does what it should. This chapter describes them.

Testing web sites and web projects

Layered applications, with display, logic, and data pieces, also seem difficult to test, especially if they're not really layered after all. This chapter explores an alternative web application design strategy that makes projects easier to maintain and easier to test, too, as well as how to test them.

Unit testing

Traditional Perl testing differs from xUnit-style testing in the way it organizes, structures, and runs tests. You can have the best of both worlds, though. This chapter discusses a Perl testing framework that allows good code reuse within object-oriented project tests and yet works within the familiar Perl testing libraries.

Testing non–Perl and non–modules

There's a whole world outside of Perl. Now that you know the power, flexibility, and ease of automated testing with Perl, this chapter suggests a few ways to use everything you've learned to test other projects written in other languages. Go forth and improve software quality worldwide.

Conventions Used in This Book

This books uses the following typographical conventions:

Italic

Used for new terms, URLs, email addresses, filenames, file extensions, pathnames, directories, and Unix utilities.

`Constant width`

Used for program listings, classes, methods, variables, keywords, and the output of commands.

`Constant width bold`

Used to show commands or other text that the user should type literally and to highlight sections of code examples.

Constant width italic
> Used to show text that should be replaced with user-supplied values.

Handwriting font
> Used for tips, suggestions, or general notes.

Using Code Examples

This book is here to help you get your job done. In general, you may use the code in this book in your programs and documentation. You do not need to contact us for permission unless you're reproducing a significant portion of the code. For example, writing a program that uses several chunks of code from this book does not require permission. Selling or distributing a CD-ROM of examples from O'Reilly books does require permission. Answering a question by citing this book and quoting example code does not require permission. Incorporating a significant amount of example code from this book into your product's documentation does require permission.

We appreciate, but do not require, attribution. An attribution usually includes the title, author, publisher, and ISBN. For example: "*Perl Testing: A Developer's Notebook*, by Ian Langworth and chromatic. Copyright 2005 O'Reilly Media, Inc., 0-596-10092-2."

If you feel your use of code examples falls outside fair use or the permission given above, feel free to contact us at *permissions@oreilly.com*.

Safari Enabled

 When you see a Safari® Enabled icon on the cover of your favorite technology book, it means the book is available online through the O'Reilly Network Safari Bookshelf.

Safari offers a solution that's better than e-books. It's a virtual library that lets you easily search thousands of top technology books, cut and paste code samples, download chapters, and find quick answers when you need the most accurate, current information. Try it for free at *http://safari.oreilly.com*.

Comments and Questions

Please address comments and questions concerning this book to the publisher:

O'Reilly Media, Inc.
1005 Gravenstein Highway North
Sebastopol, CA 95472
(800) 998-9938 (in the United States or Canada)
(707) 829-0515 (international or local)
(707) 829-0104 (fax)

We have a web page for this book, where we list errata, examples, and any additional information. You can access this page at:

> *http://www.oreilly.com/catalog/perltestingadn*

To comment or ask technical questions about this book, send email to:

> *bookquestions@oreilly.com*

For more information about our books, conferences, Resource Centers, and the O'Reilly Network, see our web site at *http://www.oreilly.com*.

The Perl QA project has a web site and mailing list devoted to discussing and improving software testing and in Perl. See the web site at *http://qa.perl.org/* for information on joining the list as well as links to other testing modules, related projects, and articles and presentations on Perl and testing.

Acknowledgments

The authors thank their editor, Allison Randal, for finding the right format for this book, for taking care of messy little details, and for weighing in with editorial advice when necessary. The authors also thank everyone in O'Reilly's production, marketing, tools, and PR groups who put this book in the hands of people who need it.

The authors also thank a bevy of technical reviewers for thoughtful suggestions, without which the book would be much poorer. In alphabetical order, they are David Adler, Ann Barcomb, Tony Bowden, Shawn Boyette, Jim Brandt, Mike Burns, Ben Evans, Shlomi Fish, Adrian Howard, Paul Johnson, James Keenan, Pete Krawczyk, Christopher Laco, Andy Lester, Pete Markowsky, Tom McTighe, Steve Peters, Curtis Poe, Steven Schubiger, Michael Schwern, Ricardo Signes, Brett Warden, and Geoffrey Young. Any remaining errors are the fault of the authors, or perhaps space aliens.

Finally, the authors thank everyone whose work has gone into the testing strategies and modules described here. Everyone's better for it.

Ian Langworth

I'd like to thank brian d foy for noticing my Perl testing quick-reference card and his initial suggestion to get the ball rolling.

Thanks to the terrific faculty and staff at the College of Computer and Information Science at Northeastern University—especially the CCIS Systems Group folks and their volunteer group, the Crew. They have provided me with an amazing community over the years, to which I owe so much. Special thanks goes to Professor Richard Rasala, who mentored me for three months in this project's early stages.

Thanks goes to Andy for all of his help and to Allison for letting this happen. Allison also set me up with a brilliant coauthor, whose grasp of the language amazes me to no end. This book wouldn't be nearly as good as it is without chromatic's tremendous writing prowess.

Thanks to all of my great friends (too many to list here), my wonderful parents, and to Emily. These people have been wonderfully supportive and deserve an immense amount of credit for having to put up with me regularly.

chromatic

Thanks to Allison for suggesting I work on this book and to Ian for coming up with the idea and accepting a coauthor. Thanks to everyone at O'Reilly for a fantastic day job. Thanks also to my friends who celebrated when I did and commiserated when I complained, especially the U of P bunch and Mel, Esther, Kate, and Eva. Apologies and love go to my family and most of all to my parents, Floyd and Annette, who know full well that I learned about testing things very early. At least now it has some productive value.

## CHAPTER 1

Beginning Testing

You've heard about the benefits of testing. You know that it can improve your code's reliability and maintainability as well as your development processes. You may even know about the wide range of available modules and idioms that Perl offers for testing Perl and non-Perl programs. In short, you may know everything except where to start.

The labs in this chapter walk through the most basic steps of running and writing automated tests with Perl. By the end of the chapter, you'll know how to start and continue testing, how Perl's testing libraries work, and where to find more libraries to ease your workload.

Installing Test Modules

One of Perl's greatest strengths is the CPAN, an archive of thousands of reusable code libraries—generally called *modules*—for almost any programming problem anyone has ever solved with Perl. This includes writing and running tests. Before you can use these modules, however, you must install them. Fortunately, Perl makes this easy.

How do I do that?

The best way to install modules from the CPAN is through a packaging system that can handle the details of finding, downloading, building, and installing the modules and their dependencies.

Through the CPAN shell

On Unix-like platforms (including Mac OS X) as well as on Windows platforms if you have a C compiler available, the easiest way to install modules is by using the CPAN module that comes with Perl. To install a new version of the Test::Simple distribution, launch the CPAN shell with the *cpan* script:

```
% cpan
cpan shell -- CPAN exploration and modules installation (v1.7601)
ReadLine support enabled

cpan> install Test::Simple
Running install for module Test::Simple
Running make for M/MS/MSCHWERN/Test-Simple-0.54.tar.gz

<...>

Appending installation info to /usr/lib/perl5/5.8.6/powerpc-linux/perllocal.
pod
  /usr/bin/make install UNINST=1 -- OK
```

You can also run the CPAN shell manually with perl -MCPAN -e shell.

If Test::Simple had any dependencies (it doesn't), the shell would have detected them and tried to install them first.

If you *haven't* used the CPAN module before, it will prompt you for all sorts of information about your machine and network configuration as well as your installation preferences. Usually the defaults are fine.

Through PPM

ActivePerl also has distributions for Linux and Solaris, so these instructions also work there.

By far, most Windows Perl installations use ActiveState's ActivePerl distribution (*http://www.activestate.com/Products/ActivePerl/*), which includes the *ppm* utility to download, configure, build, and install modules. With ActivePerl installed, open a console window and type:

```
C:\>PPM
PPM> install Test-Simple
```

If the configuration is correct, *ppm* will download and install the latest Test::Simple distribution from ActiveState's repository.

If the module that you want isn't in the repository at all or if the version in the repository is older than you like, you have a few options.

First, you can search alternate repositories. See PodMaster's list of *ppm* repositories at *http://crazyinsomniac.perlmonk.org/perl/misc/Repositories. pm*. For example, to use dada's Win32 repository permanently, use the set repository command within *ppm*:

```
C:\>PPM
PPM> set repository dada http://dada.perl.it/PPM
PPM> set save
```

By hand

If you want to install a pure-Perl module or are working on a platform that has an appropriate compiler, you can download and install the module by hand. First, find the appropriate module—perhaps by browsing *http://search.cpan.org/*. Then download the file and extract it to its own directory:

```
$ tar xvzf Test-Simple-0.54.tar.gz
Test-Simple-0.54/
<...>
```

To set up a compilation environment for Perl on Windows, consult the README.win32 file that ships with Perl.

Run the *Makefile.PL* program, and then issue the standard commands to build and test the module:

```
$ perl Makefile.PL
Checking if your kit is complete...
Looks good
Writing Makefile for Test::Simple
$ make
cp lib/Test/Builder.pm blib/lib/Test/Builder.pm
cp lib/Test/Simple.pm blib/lib/Test/Simple.pm
$ make test
```

Be sure to download the file marked This Release, not the Latest Dev. Release, unless you plan to help develop the code.

If all of the tests pass, great! Otherwise, do what you can to figure out what failed, why, and if it will hurt you. (See "Running Tests" and "Interpreting Test Results," later in this chapter, for more information.) Finally, install the module by running make install (as root, if you're installing the module system-wide).

Makefile.PL uses a module called ExtUtils::MakeMaker to configure and install other modules. Some modules use Module::Build instead of ExtUtils::MakeMaker. There are two main differences from the installation standpoint. First, they require you to have Module::Build installed. Second, the installation commands are instead:

```
$ perl Build.PL
$ perl Build
$ perl Build test
# perl Build install
```

Unix users can use ./Build instead of perl Build in the instructions.

Otherwise, they work almost identically.

Windows users may need to install Microsoft's nmake to install modules by hand. Where Unix users type make, use the nmake command instead: nmake, nmake test, and nmake install.

Consult the README.win32 file from the Perl source code distribution for links to nmake.exe.

What about...

Q: *How do I know the name to type when installing modules through PPM? I tried* install Test-More, *but it couldn't find it!*

A: Type the name of the distribution, not the module within the distribution. To find the name of the distribution, search *http://search.cpan.org/* for the name of the module that you want. In this example, Test::More is part of the Test-Simple distribution. Remove the version and use that name within PPM.

See perlfaq8 to learn more about keeping your own module directory.

Q: *I'm not an administrator on the machine, or I don't want to install the modules for everyone. How can I install a module to a specific directory?*

A: Set the PREFIX appropriately when installing the module. For example, a PREFIX of *~/perl/lib* will install these modules to that directory (at least on Unix-like machines). Then set the PERL5LIB environment variable to point there or remember to use the lib pragma to add that directory to @INC in all programs in which you want to use your locally installed modules.

MakeMaker 6.26 release will support the INSTALLBASE parameter; use that instead of PREFIX.

If you build the module by hand, run *Makefile.PL* like this:

```
$ perl Makefile.PL PREFIX=~/perl/lib
```

If you use CPAN, configure it to install modules to a directory under your control. Launch the CPAN shell with your own user account and follow the configuration questions. When it prompts for the PREFIX:

```
Every Makefile.PL is run by perl in a separate process. Likewise we
run 'make' and 'make install' in processes. If you have any
parameters (e.g. PREFIX, LIB, UNINST or the like) you want to pass
to the calls, please specify them here.

If you don't understand this question, just press ENTER.

Parameters for the 'perl Makefile.PL' command?
Typical frequently used settings:

  PREFIX=~/perl      non-root users (please see manual for more hints)

  Your choice: [ ]
```

add a prefix to a directory where you'd like to store your own modules.

If the module uses Module::Build, pass the installbase parameter instead:

```
$ perl Build.PL --installbase=~/perl
```
See the documentation for ExtUtils::MakeMaker, CPAN, and Module::Build for more details.

Running Tests

Before you can gain any benefit from writing tests, you must be able to run them. Fortunately, there are several ways to do this, depending on what you need to know.

How do I do that?

To see real tests in action, download the latest version of Test::Harness (see *http://search.cpan.org/dist/Test-Harness*) from the CPAN and extract it to its own directory. Change to this directory and build the module as usual (see "Installing Test Modules," earlier in this chapter). To run all of the tests at once, type **make test**:

```
$ make test
PERL_DL_NONLAZY=1 /usr/bin/perl5.8.6 "-MExtUtils::Command::MM" "-e" \
    "test_harness(0, 'blib/lib', 'blib/arch')" t/*.t
t/00compile.........ok 1/5# Testing Test::Harness 2.46
t/00compile.........ok
t/assert............ok
t/base..............ok
t/callback..........ok
t/harness...........ok
t/inc_taint.........ok
t/nonumbers.........ok
t/ok................ok
t/pod...............ok
t/prove-globbing....ok
t/prove-switches....ok
t/strap-analyze.....ok
t/strap.............ok
t/test-harness......ok
        56/208 skipped: various reasons
All tests successful, 56 subtests skipped.
Files=14, Tests=551,  6 wallclock secs ( 4.52 cusr +  0.97 csys =  5.49 CPU)
```

What just happened?

make test is the third step of nearly every Perl module installation. This command runs all of the test files it can find through Test::Harness, which summarizes and reports the results. It also takes care of setting the paths appropriately for as-yet-uninstalled modules.

What about...

Q: *How do I run tests for distributions that don't use Makefile.PL?*

A: `make test` comes from `ExtUtils::MakeMaker`, an old and venerable module. `Module::Build` is easier to use in some cases. If there's a *Build.PL* file, instead use the commands `perl Build.PL`, `perl Build`, and `perl Build test`. Everything will behave as described here.

Q: *How do I run tests individually?*

A: Sometimes you don't want to run everything through `make test`, as it runs all of the tests for a distribution in a specific order. If you want to run a few tests individually, use *prove* instead. It runs the test files you pass as command-line arguments, and then summarizes and prints the results.

If you don't have prove installed, you're using an old version of Test:: Harness. Use bin/ prove instead. Then upgrade.

```
$ prove t/strap*.t
t/strap-analyze....ok
t/strap............ok
All tests successful.
Files=2, Tests=284,  1 wallclock secs ( 0.66 cusr +  0.14 csys =  0.80
    CPU)
```

If you want the raw details, not just a summary, use *prove*'s verbose (-v) flag:

```
$ prove -v t/assert.t
t/assert....1..7
ok 1 - use Test::Harness::Assert;
ok 2 - assert() exported
ok 3 - assert( FALSE ) causes death
ok 4 -    with the right message
ok 5 - assert( TRUE ) does nothing
ok 6 - assert( FALSE, NAME )
ok 7 -    has the name
ok
All tests successful.
Files=1, Tests=7,  0 wallclock secs ( 0.06 cusr +  0.01 csys =  0.07
    CPU)
```

This flag prevents *prove* from eating the results. Instead, it prints them directly along with a short summary. This is very handy for development and debugging (see "Interpreting Test Results," later in this chapter).

Q: *How do I run tests individually without prove?*

A: You can run most test files manually; they're normally just Perl files.

```
$ perl t/00compile.t
1..5
ok 1 - use Test::Harness;
# Testing Test::Harness 2.42
```

```
ok 2 - use Test::Harness::Straps;
ok 3 - use Test::Harness::Iterator;
ok 4 - use Test::Harness::Assert;
ok 5 - use Test::Harness;
```

Oops! This ran the test against Test::Harness 2.42, the installed version, instead of Version 2.46, the new version. All of the other solutions set Perl's @INC path correctly. When running tests manually, use the blib module to pick up the modules as built by make or perl Build:

Confused about @INC and why it matters? See perldoc perlvar for enlightenment.

```
$ perl -Mblib t/00compile.t
1..5
ok 1 - use Test::Harness;
# Testing Test::Harness 2.46
ok 2 - use Test::Harness::Straps;
ok 3 - use Test::Harness::Iterator;
ok 4 - use Test::Harness::Assert;
ok 5 - use Test::Harness;
```

The -M switch causes Perl to load the given module just as if the program file contained a use blib; line.

The TEST_FILES argument to make_test can simplify this:

TEST_FILES can also take a file pattern, such as TEST_FILES=t/strap.t.*

```
$ make test TEST_FILES=t/00compile.t
t/00compile....ok 1/5# Testing Test::Harness 2.46
t/00compile....ok
All tests successful.
Files=1, Tests=5,  0 wallclock secs ( 0.13 cusr +  0.02 csys =  0.15
    CPU)
```

For verbose output, add TEST_VERBOSE=1.

Interpreting Test Results

Perl has a wealth of good testing modules that interoperate smoothly through a common protocol (the *Test Anything Protocol*, or *TAP*) and common libraries (Test::Builder). You'll probably never have to write your own testing protocol, but understanding TAP will help you interpret your test results and write better tests.

All of the test modules in this book produce TAP output. Test::Harness interprets that output. Think of it as a minilanguage about test successes and failures.

How do I do that?

Save the following program to *sample_output.pl*:

```
#!perl

print <<END_HERE;
1..9
ok 1
not ok 2
```

Using Windows and seeing an error about END_HERE? Add a newline to the end of sample_output. pl, then read perldoc perlfaq8.

```
#     Failed test (t/sample_output.t at line 10)
#          got: '2'
#     expected: '4'
ok 3
ok 4 - this is test 4
not ok 5 - test 5 should look good too
not ok 6 # TODO fix test 6
# I haven't had time add the feature for test 6
ok 7 # skip these tests never pass in examples
ok 8 # skip these tests never pass in examples
ok 9 # skip these tests never pass in examples
END_HERE
```

Now run it through *prove* (see "Running Tests," earlier in this chapter):

```
$ prove sample_output.pl
sample_output....FAILED tests 2, 5
    Failed 2/9 tests, 77.789 okay (less 3 skipped tests: 4 okay, 44.44%)
Failed Test       Stat Wstat Total Fail  Failed  List of Failed
-----------------------------------------------------------------------
sample_output.pl                9    2 22.22%  2 5
3 subtests skipped.
Failed 1/1 test scripts, 0.00% okay. 2/9 subtests failed, 77.79% okay.
```

What just happened?

prove interpreted the output of the script as it would the output of a real test. In fact, there's no effective difference—a real test might produce that exact output.

The lines of the test correspond closely to the results. The first line of the output is the test plan. In this case, it tells the harness to plan to run 9 tests. The second line of the report shows that 9 tests ran, but two failed: tests 2 and 5, both of which start with not ok.

The report also mentions three skipped tests. These are tests 7 through 9, all of which contain the text # skip. They count as successes, not failures. (See "Skipping Tests" in Chapter 2 to learn why.)

That leaves one curious line, test 6. It starts with not ok, but it does not count as a failure because of the text # TODO. The test author expected this test to fail but left it in and marked it appropriately. (See "Marking Tests as TODO" in Chapter 2.)

The test harness ignored all of the rest of the output, which consists of developer diagnostics. When developing, it's often useful to look at the test output in its entirety, whether by using prove -v or running the tests directly through perl (see "Running Tests," earlier in this chapter). This prevents the harness from suppressing the diagnostic output, as found with the second test in the sample output.

What about...

Q: *What happens when the actual number of tests is different than expected?*

A: Running the wrong number of tests counts as a failure. Save the following test as *too_few_tests.t*:

```
use Test::More tests => 3;

pass( 'one test'  );
pass( 'two tests' );
```

Run it with *prove*:

```
$ prove too_few_tests.t
too_few_tests....ok 2/3# Looks like you planned 3 tests but only ran 2.
too_few_tests....dubious
        Test returned status 1 (wstat 256, 0x100)
DIED. FAILED test 3
        Failed 1/3 tests, 66.67% okay
Failed Test     Stat Wstat Total Fail  Failed  List of Failed
-------------------------------------------------------------------------
too_few_tests.t   1   256     3    2 66.67% 3
Failed 1/1 test scripts, 0.00% okay. 1/3 subtests failed, 66.67% okay.
```

Test::More complained about the mismatch between the test plan and the number of tests that actually ran. The same goes for running too many tests. Save the following code as *too_many_tests.t*:

```
use Test::More tests => 2;

pass( 'one test'    );
pass( 'two tests'   );
pass( 'three tests' );
```

Run it with *prove*:

```
$ prove -v too_many_tests.t
too_many_tests....ok 3/2# Looks like you planned 2 tests but ran 1
extra.
too_many_tests....dubious
        Test returned status 1 (wstat 256, 0x100)
DIED. FAILED test 3
        Failed 1/2 tests, 50.00% okay
Failed Test     Stat Wstat Total Fail  Failed  List of Failed
-------------------------------------------------------------------------
too_many_tests.t   1   256     2    1 50.00% 3
Failed 1/1 test scripts, 0.00% okay. -1/2 subtests failed, 150.00% okay.
```

This time, the harness interpreted the presence of the third test as a failure and reported it as such. Again, Test::More warned about the mismatch.

Writing Your First Test

This lab introduces the most basic features of Test::Simple, the simplest testing module. You'll see how to write your own test for a simple "Hello, world!"–style program.

How do I do that?

Open your favorite text editor and create a file called *hello.t*. Enter the following code:

```perl
#!perl

use strict;
use warnings;

use Test::Simple tests => 1;

sub hello_world
{
    return "Hello, world!";
}

ok( hello_world() eq "Hello, world!" );
```

Save it. Now you have a simple Perl test file. Run it from the command line with *prove*:

```
$ prove hello.t
```

You'll see the following output:

```
hello....ok
All tests successful.
Files=1, Tests=1,  0 wallclock secs ( 0.09 cusr +  0.00 csys =  0.09 CPU)
```

What just happened?

hello.t looks like a normal Perl program; it uses a couple of pragmas to catch misbehavior as well as the Test::Simple module. It defines a simple subroutine. There's no special syntax a decent Perl programmer doesn't already know.

The first potential twist is the use of Test::Simple. By convention, all test files need a plan to declare how many tests you expect to run. If you run the test file with *perl* and not *prove*, you'll notice that the plan output comes before the test output:

```
$ perl hello.t
1..1
ok 1
```

The other interesting piece is the ok( ) subroutine. It comes from Test::Simple and is the module's only export. ok( ) is very, very simple. It reports a passed or a failed test, depending on the truth of its first argument. In the example, if whatever hello_world( ) returns is equal to the string Hello, world!, ok( ) will report that the test has passed.

Anything that can go in an if statement is fair game for ok( ).

As the output shows, there's one test in the file, and it passed. Congratulations!

What about...

Q: *How do I avoid changing the plan number every time I add a test?*

A: Writing 'no_plan' on the use line lets Test::Simple know that you're playing it by ear. In this case, it'll keep its own count of tests and report that you ran as many as you ran.

In some cases, the number of tests you run is important, so providing a real plan is a good habit to cultivate.

```perl
#!perl

use strict;
use warnings;

use Test::Simple 'no_plan';

sub hello_world
{
    return "Hello, world!";
}

ok( hello_world() eq "Hello, world!" );
```

When you declare no_plan, the test plan comes after the test output.

```
$ perl hello.t
ok 1
1..1
```

This is very handy for developing, when you don't know how many tests you'll add. Having a plan is a nice sanity check against unexpected occurrences, though, so consider switching back to using a plan when you finish adding a batch of tests.

Q: *How do I make it easier to track down which tests are failing?*

A: When there are multiple tests in a file and some of them fail, descriptions help to explain what should have happened. Hopefully that will help you track down *why* the tests failed. It's easy to add a description; just change the ok line.

```
ok( hello_world() eq "Hello, world!",
    'hello_world() output should be sane' );
```

You should see the same results as before when running it through *prove*. Running it with the verbose flag will show the test description:

```
$ prove -v hello.t
1..1
ok 1 - hello_world() output should be sane
```

Q: *How do I make more detailed comparisons?*

A: Don't worry; though you can define an entire test suite in terms of ok( ), dozens of powerful and freely available testing modules work together nicely to provide much more powerful testing functions. That list starts with the aptly named Test::More.

Loading Modules

Most of the Perl testing libraries assume that you use them to test Perl modules. Modules are the building blocks of larger Perl programs and well-designed code uses them appropriately. Loading modules for testing seems simple, but it has two complications: how do you know you've loaded the right version of the module you want to test, and how do you know that you've loaded it successfully?

This lab explains how to test both questions, with a little help from Test::More.

How do I do that?

Imagine that you're developing a module to analyze sentences to prove that so-called professional writers have poor grammar skills. You've started by writing a module named AnalyzeSentence that performs some basic word counting. Save the following code in your library directory as *AnalyzeSentence.pm*:

```
package AnalyzeSentence;

use strict;
use warnings;

use base 'Exporter';

our $WORD_SEPARATOR = qr/\s+/;
our @EXPORT_OK      = qw( $WORD_SEPARATOR count_words words );
```

```perl
sub words
{
    my $sentence = shift;
    return split( $WORD_SEPARATOR, $sentence );
}

sub count_words
{
    my $sentence = shift;
    return scalar words( $sentence );
}

1;
```

Besides checking that words() and count_words() do the right thing, a good test should test that the module loads and imports the two subroutines correctly. Save the following test file as *analyze_sentence.t*:

```perl
#!perl

use strict;
use warnings;

use Test::More tests => 5;

my @subs = qw( words count_words );

use_ok( 'AnalyzeSentence', @subs    );
can_ok( __PACKAGE__, 'words'        );
can_ok( __PACKAGE__, 'count_words'  );

my $sentence =
    'Queen Esther, ruler of the Frog-Human Alliance, briskly devours a
    monumental ice cream sundae in her honor.';

my @words = words( $sentence );
ok( @words == 17, 'words() should return all words in sentence' );

$sentence = 'Rampaging ideas flutter greedily.';
my $count = count_words( $sentence );

ok( $count == 4, 'count_words() should handle simple sentences' );
```

Run it with *prove*:

```
$ prove analyze_sentence.t
analyze_sentence....ok
All tests successful.
Files=1, Tests=5,  0 wallclock secs ( 0.08 cusr +  0.01 csys =  0.09 CPU)
```

What just happened?

Instead of starting with Test::Simple, the test file uses Test::More. As the name suggests, Test::More does everything that Test::Simple does—and more! In particular, it provides the use_ok( ) and can_ok( ) functions shown in the test file.

See perldoc perlmod and perldoc -f use to learn more about import( ).

use_ok( ) takes the name of a module to load, AnalyzeSentence in this case, and an optional list of symbols to pass to the module's import( ) method. It attempts to load the module and import the symbols and passes or fails a test based on the results. It's the test equivalent of writing:

```
use AnalyzeSentence qw( words count_words );
```

can_ok( ) is the test equivalent of the can( ) method. The tests use it here to see if the module has exported words( ) and count_words( ) functions into the current namespace. These tests aren't *entirely* necessary, as the ok( ) functions later in the file will fail if the functions are missing, but the import tests can fail for only two reasons: either the import has failed or someone mistyped their names in the test file.

See perldoc UNIVERSAL to learn more about can( ).

What about...

Q: *I don't want to use* use; *I want to use* require. *Can I do that? How?*

A: See the Test::More documentation for require_ok( ).

Q: *What if I need to import symbols from the module as it loads?*

A: If the test file depends on variables defined in the module being tested, for example, wrap the use_ok( ) line in a BEGIN block. Consider adding tests for the behavior of $WORD_SEPARATOR. Modify the use_ok( ) line and add the following lines to the end of *analyze_sentence.t*:

```
use_ok( 'AnalyzeSentence', @subs, '$WORD_SEPARATOR' ) or exit;

...

$WORD_SEPARATOR = qr/(?:\s|-)+/;
@words    = words( $sentence );
ok( @words == 18, '... respecting $WORD_SEPARATOR, if set' );
```

Run the test:

```
$ prove t/analyze_sentence.t
t/analyze_sentence....Global symbol "$WORD_SEPARATOR" requires explicit
    package name at t/analyze_sentence.t line 28.
Execution of t/analyze_sentence.t aborted due to compilation errors.
# Looks like your test died before it could output anything.
t/analyze_sentence....dubious
    Test returned status 255 (wstat 65280, 0xff00)
        FAILED--1 test script could be run, alas--no output ever seen
```

With the strict pragma enabled, when Perl reaches the last lines of the test file in its compile stage, it hasn't seen the variable named

$WORD_SEPARATOR yet. Only when it runs the use_ok( ) line at runtime will it import the variable.

Change the use_ok( ) line once more:

```
BEGIN { use_ok( 'AnalyzeSentence', @subs, '$WORD_SEPARATOR') or exit;}
```

Then run the test again:

```
$ prove t/analyze_sentence.t
t/analyze_sentence....ok
All tests successful.
Files=1, Tests=6,  0 wallclock secs ( 0.09 cusr +  0.00 csys =  0.09
    CPU)
```

See perldoc perlmod for more information about BEGIN and compile time.

Q: *What if Perl can't find AnalyzeSentence or it fails to compile?*

A: If there's a syntax error somewhere in the module, some of your tests will pass and others will fail mysteriously. The successes and failures depend on what Perl has already compiled by the time it reaches the error. It's difficult to recover from this kind of failure.

The best thing you can do may be to quit the test altogether:

```
use_ok( 'AnalyzeSentence' ) or exit;
```

If you've specified a plan, Test::Harness will note the mismatch between the number of tests run (probably one) and the number of tests expected. Either way, it's much easier to see the compilation failure if it's the last failure reported.

Some testers prefer to use die( ) with an informative error message.

Improving Test Comparisons

ok( ) may be the basis of all testing, but it can be inconvenient to have to reduce every test in your system to a single conditional expression. Fortunately, Test::More provides several other testing functions that can make your work easier. You'll likely end up using these functions more often than ok( ).

This lab demonstrates how to use the most common testing functions found in Test::More.

How do I do that?

The following listing tests a class named Greeter, which takes the name and age of a person and allows her to greet other people. Save this code as *greeter.t*:

```
#!perl

use strict;
```

The examples in "Writing Your First Test," earlier in this chapter, will work the same way if you substitute Test::More for Test::Simple; Test::More is a superset of Test:: Simple.

```
use warnings;

use Test::More tests => 4;

use_ok( 'Greeter' ) or exit;

my $greeter = Greeter->new( name => 'Emily', age => 21 );
isa_ok( $greeter, 'Greeter' );

is(   $greeter->age(),   21,
    'age() should return age for object' );
like( $greeter->greet(), qr/Hello, .+ is Emily!/,
    'greet() should include object name' );
```

Now save the module being tested in your library directory as *Greeter.pm*:

```
package Greeter;

sub new
{
    my ($class, %args) = @_;
    bless \%args, $class;
}

sub name
{
    my $self = shift;
    return $self->{name};
}

sub age
{
    my $self = shift;
    return $self->{age};
}

sub greet
{
    my $self = shift;
    return "Hello, my name is " . $self->name() . "!";
}

1;
```

Running the file from the command line with *prove* should reveal three successful tests:

```
$ prove greeter.t
greeter.t....ok
All tests successful.
Files=1, Tests=4,  0 wallclock secs ( 0.07 cusr +  0.03 csys =  0.10 CPU)
```

What just happened?

This program starts by loading the Greeter module and creating a new Greeter object for Emily, age 21. The first test checks to see if the constructor returned an actual Greeter object. isa_ok() performs several checks to see if the variable is actually a defined reference, for example. It fails if it is an undefined value, a non-reference, or an object of any class other than the appropriate class or a derived class.

The next test checks that the object's age matches the age set for Emily in the constructor. Where a test using Test::Simple would have to perform this comparison manually, Test::More provides the is() function that takes two arguments to compare, along with the test description. It compares the values, reporting a successful test if they match and a failed test if they don't.

Similarly, the final test uses like() to compare the first two arguments. The second argument is a regular expression compiled with the qr// operator. like() compares this regular expression against the first argument—in this case, the result of the call to $greeter->greet()—and reports a successful test if it matches and a failed test if it doesn't.

Avoiding the need to write the comparisons manually is helpful, but the real improvement in this case is how these functions behave when tests fail. Add two more tests to the file and remember to change the test plan to declare six tests instead of four. The new code is:

```
use Test::More tests => 6;

...

is(  $greeter->age(),    22,
    'Emily just had a birthday' );
like( $greeter->greet(), qr/Howdy, pardner!/,
    '... and she talks like a cowgirl' );
```

Run the tests again with *prove*'s verbose mode:

```
$ prove -v greeter.t
greeter.t....1..6
ok 1 - use Greeter;
ok 2 - The object isa Greeter
ok 3 - age() should return age for object
ok 4 - greet() should include object name
not ok 5 - Emily just had a birthday
#     Failed test (greeter.t at line 18)
#          got: '21'
#     expected: '22'
not ok 6 - ... and she talks like a cowgirl
#     Failed test (greeter.t at line 20)
#                   'Hello, my name is Emily!'
```

Test::More::is() uses a string comparison. This isn't always the right choice for your data. See Test::More::cmp_ok() to perform other comparisons.

See "Regexp Quote-Like Operators" in perlop to learn more about qr//.

```
#       doesn't match '(?-xism:Howdy, pardner!)'
# Looks like you failed 2 tests of 6.
dubious
        Test returned status 2 (wstat 512, 0x200)
DIED. FAILED tests 5-6
        Failed 2/6 tests, 66.67% okay
Failed Test Stat Wstat Total Fail  Failed  List of Failed
-------------------------------------------------------------------------------
greeter.t    2   512     6    2  33.33% 5-6
Failed 1/1 test scripts, 0.00% okay. 2/6 subtests failed, 66.67% okay.
```

The current version of prove doesn't display the descriptions of failing tests, but it does display diagnostic output.

Notice that the output for the new tests—those that shouldn't pass—contains debugging information, including what the test saw, what it expected to see, and the line number of the test. If there's only one benefit to using ok() from Test::Simple or Test::More, it's these diagnostics.

What about...

Q: *How do I test things that shouldn't match?*

A: Test::More provides isnt() and unlike(), which work the same way as is() and like(), except that the tests pass if the arguments *do not* match. Changing the fourth test to use isnt() and the fifth test to use unlike() will make them pass, though the test descriptions will seem weird.

## CHAPTER 2

Writing Tests

Perl has a rich vocabulary, but you can accomplish many things using only a fraction of the power available. In the same way, Perl has an ever-increasing number of testing modules and best practices built around the simple ok( ) function described in Chapter 1.

The labs in this chapter guide you through the advanced features of Test::More and other commonly used testing modules. You'll learn how to control which tests run and why, how to compare expected and received data effectively, and how to test exceptional conditions. These are crucial techniques that provide the building blocks for writing comprehensive test suites.

Skipping Tests

Some tests should run only under certain conditions. For example, a network test to an external service makes sense only if an Internet connection is available, or an OS-specific test may run only on a certain platform. This lab shows how to skip tests that you know will never pass.

How do I do that?

Suppose that you're writing an English-to-Dutch translation program. The Phrase class stores some text and provides a constructor, an accessor, and an as_dutch( ) method that returns the text translated to Dutch.

Save the following code as *Phrase.pm*:

```perl
package Phrase;
use strict;

sub new
{
```

```
        my ( $class, $text ) = @_;
        bless \$text, $class;
}

sub text
{
    my $self = shift;
    return $$self;
}

sub as_dutch
{
    my $self = shift;
    require WWW::Babelfish;
    return WWW::Babelfish->new->translate(
        source      => 'English',
        destination => 'Dutch',
        text        => $self->text(),
    );
}

1;
```

A user may or may not have the WWW::Babelfish translation module installed. That's fine; you've decided that Phrase's as_dutch( ) feature is optional. How can you test that, though?

Save the following code as *phrase.t*:

```
#!perl

use strict;

use Test::More tests => 3;
use Phrase;

my $phrase = Phrase->new('Good morning!');
isa_ok( $phrase, 'Phrase' );

is( $phrase->text(), 'Good morning!', "text() access works" );

SKIP:
{
    eval 'use WWW::Babelfish';

    skip( 'because WWW::Babelfish required for as_dutch()', 1 ) if $@;

    is(
        $phrase->as_dutch,
        'Goede ochtend!',
        "successfully translated to Dutch"
      );
}
```

Run the test file with *prove* in verbose mode. If you have WWW::Babelfish installed, you will see the following output:

```
$ prove -v phrase.t
phrase....1..3
ok 1 - The object isa Phrase
ok 2 - text( ) access works
ok 3 - successfully translated to Dutch
ok
All tests successful.
Files=1, Tests=3,  1 wallclock secs ( 0.16 cusr +  0.01 csys =  0.17 CPU)
```

If you run the test *without* WWW::Babelfish, you will see a different result:

```
$ prove -v phrase.t
phrase....1..3
ok 1 - The object isa Phrase
ok 2 - text( ) access works
ok 3 # skip because WWW::Babelfish required for as_dutch( )
ok
        1/3 skipped: because WWW::Babelfish required for as_dutch( )
All tests successful, 1 subtest skipped.
Files=1, Tests=3,  0 wallclock secs ( 0.02 cusr +  0.00 csys =  0.02 CPU)
```

What just happened?

The test file begins with a Test::More declaration, as you've seen in the previous labs. The test file creates a sample Phrase object and also tests its constructor and text( ) accessor.

To skip the test for as_dutch( ) if the user does not have the WWW::Babelfish module installed requires a bit of special syntax. The test has a single block labeled SKIP, which begins by attempting to load the WWW::Babelfish module.

You can have as many blocks labeled SKIP as you need. You can even nest them, as long as you label every nested block SKIP as well.

If trying to use WWW::Babelfish fails, eval will catch such an error and put it in the global variable $@. Otherwise, it will clear that variable. If there's something in $@, the function on the next line executes. skip( ), yet another function helpfully exported by Test::More, takes two arguments: the reason to give for skipping the tests and the number of tests to skip. The previous case skips one test, explaining that the optional module is not available.

Even though the test for as_dutch( ) did not run, it counts as a success because marking it as a skipped test means that you expect it will *never* run under the given circumstances. If WWW::Babelfish *were* available, the test would run normally and its success or failure would count as a normal test.

Test::Harness reports all skipped tests as successes because it's behavior that you anticipated.

Skipping All Tests

The preceding lab demonstrated how to skip certain tests under certain conditions. You may find cases where an entire test *file* shouldn't run—for example, when testing platform X–specific features on platform Y will produce no meaningful results. `Test::More` provides a bit of useful syntax for this situation.

How do I do that?

Use the `plan` function on its own instead of specifying the tests in the `use( )` statement. The following code checks to see if the current weekday is Tuesday. If it is not, the test will skip all of the tests. Save it as *skip_all.t*:

```
use Test::More;

if ( [ localtime ]->[6] != 2 )
{
    plan( skip_all => 'only run these tests on Tuesday' );
}
else
{
    plan( tests => 1 );
}

require Tuesday;
my $day = Tuesday->new( );
ok( $day->coat( ), 'we brought our coat' );
```

Tuesday.pm is very simple:

```
package Tuesday;

sub new
{
    bless {}, shift;
}

# wear a coat only on Tuesday
sub coat
{
    return [ localtime ]->[6] == 2;
}

1;
```

Run this test file on a Tuesday to see the following output:

```
$ prove -v skip_all.t
chapter_01/skipping_all_tests....1..1
ok 1 - we brought our coat
```

```
ok
All tests successful.
Files=1, Tests=1,  1 wallclock secs ( 0.13 cusr +  0.04 csys =  0.17 CPU)
```

Run it on any other day of the week to skip all of the tests:

```
$ prove -v skip_all.t
chapter_01/skipping_all_tests....1..0 # Skip only run these tests on Tuesday
skipped
        all skipped: only run these tests on Tuesday
All tests successful, 1 test skipped.
Files=1, Tests=0,  0 wallclock secs ( 0.14 cusr +  0.05 csys =  0.19 CPU)
```

A real test file
would have more
tests; this is just
an example.

What just happened?

Instead of immediately reporting the test plan by passing extra arguments to the use keyword, *skip_all.t* uses Test::More's plan( ) function
to determine the test plan when the script runs. If the current weekday is
not Tuesday, the code calls plan( ) with two arguments: an instruction to
run no tests and a reason why. If it *is* Tuesday, the code reports the regular test plan and execution continues as normal.

Marking Tests as TODO

Even though having a well-tested codebase can increase your development speed, you may still have more features to add and bugs to fix than
you can program in the current session. It can be useful to capture this
information in tests, though they'll obviously fail because there's no code
yet! Fortunately, you can mark these tasks as executable, testable TODO
items that your test harness will track for you until you get around to fin-
ishing them.

How do I do that?

Take a good idea for some code: a module that reads future versions of
files. That will be really useful. Call it File::Future, and save the following code to *File/Future.pm*, creating the *File/* directory first if necessary:

```
package File::Future;

use strict;

sub new
{
    my ($class, $filename) = @_;
    bless { filename => $filename }, $class;
}
```

```
sub retrieve
{
    # implement later...
}

1;
```

The `File::Future` constructor takes a file path and returns an object. Calling `retrieve()` on the object with a date retrieves that file at the given date. Unfortunately, there is no Perl extension to flux capacitors yet. For now, hold off on writing the implementation of `retrieve()`.

There's no sense in not testing the code, though. It'll be nice to know that the code does what it needs to do by whatever Christmas `Acme::FluxFS` finally appears. It's easy to test that. Save the following code as *future.t*:

```
use Test::More tests => 4;
use File::Future;

my $file = File::Future->new( 'perl_testing_dn.pod' );
isa_ok( $file, 'File::Future' );

TODO: {
    local $TODO = 'continuum not yet harnessed';

    ok( my $current = $file->retrieve( 'January 30, 2005' ) );
    ok( my $future  = $file->retrieve( 'January 30, 2070' ) );

    cmp_ok( length($current), '<', length($future),
        'ensuring that we have added text by 2070' );
}
```

Run the test with *prove*. It will produce the following output:

```
$ prove -v future.t
future.t....1..4
ok 1 - The object isa File::Future
not ok 2 # TODO continuum not yet harnessed
#     Failed (TODO) test (future.t.pl at line 14)
not ok 3 # TODO continuum not yet harnessed
#     Failed (TODO) test (future.t.pl at line 15)
not ok 4 - ensuring that we have added text by 2070 # TODO
        continuum not yet harnessed
#     Failed (TODO) test (future.t at line 13)
#     '0'
#          <
#     '0'
ok
All tests successful.
Files=1, Tests=4,  0 wallclock secs ( 0.02 cusr +  0.00 csys =  0.02 CPU)
```

What just happened?

The test file for `File::Future` marks the tests for retrieval of documents from the future as an unfinished, but planned, feature.

To mark a set of tests as TODO items, put them in a block labeled TODO, similar to the `SKIP` block from "Skipping Tests," earlier in this chapter. Instead of using a function similar to `skip()`, localize the $TODO variable and assign it a string containing the reason that the tests should not pass.

Notice in the previous output that `Test::More` labeled the tests with TODO messages and the TODO reason. The TODO tests fail, but because the test file set that expectation, the test harness considers them successful tests anyway.

Unlike skipped tests, tests marked as TODO do actually run. However, unlike regular tests, the test harness interprets failing TODOs as a success.

What about...

Q: *What happens if the tests succeed? For example, if the tests exercise a bug and someone fixes it while fixing something else, what will happen?*

A: If the tests marked as TODO do in fact pass, the diagnostics from the test harness will report that some tests unexpectedly succeeded:

```
$ prove -v future.t
future-pass....1..4
ok 1 - The object isa File::Future
ok 2 # TODO continuum not yet harnessed
ok 3 # TODO continuum not yet harnessed
ok 4 # TODO continuum not yet harnessed
ok
        3/4 unexpectedly succeeded
All tests successful (3 subtests UNEXPECTEDLY SUCCEEDED).
Files=1, Tests=4,  0 wallclock secs ( 0.02 cusr +  0.00 csys =  0.02
    CPU)
```

This is good; you can then move the passing tests out of the TODO block and promote them to full-fledged tests that should always pass.

Simple Data Structure Equality

`Test::More`'s `is()` function checks scalar equality, but what about more complicated structures, such as lists of lists of lists? Good tests often need to peer into these data structures to test whether, deep down inside, they are truly equal. The first solution that may come to mind is a recursive function or a series of nested loops. Hold that thought, though—Test::More and other test modules provide a better way with their comparison functions.

How do I do that?

Save this code as *deeply.t*:

```
use Test::More tests => 1;

my $list1 =
[
    [
        [ 48, 12 ],
        [ 32, 10 ],
    ],
    [
        [ 03, 28 ],
    ],
];

my $list2 =
[
    [
        [ 48, 12 ],
        [ 32, 11 ],
    ],
    [
        [ 03, 28 ],
    ],
];

is_deeply( $list1, $list2, 'existential equivalence' );
```

Run it with prove -v to see the diagnostics:

```
$ prove -v deeply.t
deeply....1..1
not ok 1 - existential equivalence
#     Failed test (deeply.t at line 23)
#     Structures begin differing at:
#          $got->[0][1][1] = '10'
#     $expected->[0][1][1] = '11'
# Looks like you failed 1 tests of 1.
dubious
   Test returned status 1 (wstat 256, 0x100)
DIED. FAILED test 1
   Failed 1/1 tests, 0.00% okay
Failed 1/1 test scripts, 0.00% okay. 1/1 subtests failed, 0.00% okay.
Failed Test Stat Wstat Total Fail  Failed  List of Failed
-------------------------------------------------------------------------
deeply.t      1   256     1    1 100.00%  1
```

What just happened?

The example test compares two lists of lists with the is_deeply() function exported by Test::More. Note the difference between the two lists. Because the first array contains a 10 where the second contains an 11, the test failed.

The output shows the difference between $list1 and $list2. If there are multiple differences in the data structure, is_deeply() will display only the first. Additionally, if one of the data structures is missing an element, is_deeply() will show that as well.

What about...

Q: *How do I see the differences, but not the similarities, between data structures in my test output?*

A: Test::Differences exports a function, eq_or_diff( ), that shows a Unix diff-like output for data structures. *differences.t* is a modified version of the previous test file that uses this function.

```
use Test::More tests => 1;
use Test::Differences;

my $list1 = [
    [
        [ 48, 12 ],
        [ 32, 10 ],
    ],
    [
        [ 03, 28 ],
    ],
];

my $list2 = [
    [
        [ 48, 12 ],
        [ 32, 11 ],
    ],
    [
        [ 03, 28 ],
    ],
];

eq_or_diff( $list1, $list2, 'a tale of two references' );
```

Running the file with *prove* produces the following output. Diagnostic lines beginning and ending with an asterisk (*) mark where the data structures differ.

```
$ prove -v differences.t
differences....1..1
not ok 1 - a tale of two references
#     Failed test (differences.t at line 24)
# +----+-----------+-----------+
# | Elt|Got        |Expected   |
# +----+-----------+-----------+
# |   0|[          |[          |
# |   1|  [        |  [        |
# |   2|    [      |    [      |
# |   3|      48,  |      48,  |
# |   4|      12   |      12   |
# |   5|    ],     |    ],     |
# |   6|    [      |    [      |
# |   7|      32,  |      32,  |
# * 8|      10   |      11   *
# |   9|    ]      |    ]      |
# |  10|  ],       |  ],       |
# |  11|  [        |  [        |
# |  12|    [      |    [      |
# |  13|      3,   |      3,   |
# |  14|      28   |      28   |
# |  15|    ]      |    ]      |
# |  16|  ]        |  ]        |
# |  17|]          |]          |
# +----+-----------+-----------+
# Looks like you failed 1 tests of 1.
dubious
  Test returned status 1 (wstat 256, 0x100)
DIED. FAILED test 1
  Failed 1/1 tests, 0.00% okay
Failed 1/1 test scripts, 0.00% okay. 1/1 subtests failed, 0.00% okay.
Failed Test   Stat Wstat Total Fail  Failed  List of Failed
-------------------------------------------------------------------
differences.t    1   256     1    1 100.00%  1
```

Q: *How do I compare two strings, line-by-line?*

A: Test::Differences shows the difference between multiline strings with its eq_or_diff( ) function. The following example tests the equality of two multiline strings using eq_or_diff( ). Save it as *strings.t*:

```
use Test::More tests => 1;
use Test::Differences;

my $string1 = <<"END1";
Lorem ipsum dolor sit
amet, consectetuer
adipiscing elit.
END1

my $string2 = <<"END2";
Lorem ipsum dolor sit
amet, facilisi
```

```
adipiscing elit.
END2

eq_or_diff( $string1, $string2, 'are they the same?' );
```

Running it with *prove* produces the following output:

```
$ prove -v strings.t
strings....1..1
not ok 1 - are they the same?
#      Failed test (strings.t at line 16)
# +---+-----------------------+-----------------------+
# | Ln|Got                    |Expected               |
# +---+-----------------------+-----------------------+
# |   1|Lorem ipsum dolor sit |Lorem ipsum dolor sit  |
# * 2|amet, consectetuer     |amet, facilisi         *
# |   3|adipiscing elit.      |adipiscing elit.       |
# +---+-----------------------+-----------------------+
# Looks like you failed 1 tests of 1.
dubious
  Test returned status 1 (wstat 256, 0x100)
DIED. FAILED test 1
  Failed 1/1 tests, 0.00% okay
Failed 1/1 test scripts, 0.00% okay. 1/1 subtests failed, 0.00% okay.
Failed Test Stat Wstat Total Fail  Failed  List of Failed
-----------------------------------------------------------------------
strings.t      1   256     1    1 100.00% 1
```

The diagnostics resemble those from *differences.t,* with differing lines in the multiline string marked with asterisks.

Q: *How do I compare binary data?*

A: It's useful to see escape sequences of some sort in the differences, which is precisely what the Test::LongString module does. Test:: LongString provides a handful of useful functions for comparing and testing strings that are not in plain text or are especially long.

Modify *strings.t* to use the is_string() function, and save it as *longstring.t:*

```
use Test::More tests => 1;
use Test::LongString;

my $string1 = <<"END1";
Lorem ipsum dolor sit
amet, consectetuer
adipiscing elit.
END1

my $string2 = <<"END2";
Lorem ipsum dolor sit
amet, facilisi
adipiscing elit.
END2
```

```
                    is_string( $string1, $string2, 'are they the same?' );
```
Run *longstring.t* using *prove* to see the following:

*Test::LongString
also exports other
handy string-
testing functions
that produce
similar diagnostic
output. See the
module's documen-
tation for more
information.*

```
$ prove -v longstring.t
longstring....1..1
not ok 1 - are they the same?
#     Failed test (longstring.t at line 16)
#          got: "Lorem ipsum dolor sit \x{0a}amet, consectetuer \
x{0a}adipisc"...
#        length: 61
#     expected: "Lorem ipsum dolor sit \x{0a}amet, facilisi \
x{0a}adipiscing "...
#        length: 57
#     strings begin to differ at char 23
# Looks like you failed 1 tests of 1.
dubious
  Test returned status 1 (wstat 256, 0x100)
DIED. FAILED test 1
  Failed 1/1 tests, 0.00% okay
Failed 1/1 test scripts, 0.00% okay. 1/1 subtests failed, 0.00% okay.
Failed Test  Stat Wstat Total Fail  Failed  List of Failed
-------------------------------------------------------------------------
longstring.t   1   256     1    1 100.00%  1
```

*\x{0a} is one way
to represent the
newline character.*

The diagnostic output from Test::LongString's is_string( ) escapes nonprinting characters (\x{0a}), shows the length of each string (61 and 57), and shows the position of the first different character.

Data Composition

As the data structures your code uses become more complex, so will your tests. It's important to verify what actually makes up a data structure instead of simply comparing it to an existing structure. You *could* iterate through each level of a complex nested hash of arrays, checking each and every element. Fortunately, the Test::Deep module neatens up code testing complicated data structures and provides sensible error messages.

How do I do that?

Save the following as *cmp_deeply.t*:

```
use Test::More tests => 1;
use Test::Deep;

my $points =
[
    { x => 50, y =>  75 },
    { x => 19, y => -29 },
];
```

```
my $is_integer = re('^-?\d+$');

cmp_deeply( $points,
  array_each(
    {
      x => $is_integer,
      y => $is_integer,
    }
  ),
          'both sets of points should be integers' );
```

Now run *cmp_deeply.t* from the command line with *prove*. It will show one successful test:

```
$ prove cmp_deeply.t
cmp_deep....ok
All tests successful.
Files=1, Tests=1,  0 wallclock secs ( 0.06 cusr +  0.00 csys =  0.06 CPU)
```

What just happened?

cmp_deeply( ), like most other testing functions, accepts two or three arguments: the data structure to test, what you expect the structure to look like, and an optional test description. The expected data, however, is a special test structure with a format containing special Test::Deep functions.

The test file begins by creating a regular expression using re( ), a function exported by Test::Deep. re( ) declares that the data must match the given regular expression. If you use a regular expression reference instead, Test::Deep believes you expect the data to *be* a regular expression instead of matching the data against it.

re( ) also lets you perform checks on the data it matches. See the Test::Deep documentation for details.

Test::Deep's array_each( ) function creates the main test structure for the test. To pass the test, $points must be an array reference. Every element of the array must validate against the test structure passed to array_each( ).

Passing a hash reference as the test structure declares that every element must be a hash reference and the values of the given hash must match the values in the test structure's hash. In *cmp_deeply.t*, the hash contains only two keys, x and y, so the given hash must contain only those keys. Additionally, both values must match the regular expression created with re( ).

Test::Deep's diagnostics are really useful with large data structures. Change $points so that the y value of the first hash is the letter "Q", which is invalid according to the provided test structure. Save it as *cmp_deeply2.t*:

```
use Test::More tests => 1;
use Test::Deep;

my $points =
[
    { x => 50, y => 75 },
    { x => 19, y => 'Q' },
];

my $is_integer = re('^-?\d+$');

cmp_deeply( $points,
  array_each(
    {
      x => $is_integer,
      y => $is_integer,
    }
  )
);
```

Now run *cmp_deeply2.t* with `prove -v`. The `cmp_deeply( )` function will fail with the following diagnostic:

```
$ prove -v cmp_deeply2.t
-cmp_deep2....#     Failed test (cmp_deep2.t at line 11)
# Using Regexp on $points->[1]{"y"}
#     got : 'Q'
# expect : (?-xism:^-?\d+$)
# Looks like you failed 1 tests of 1.
dubious
    Test returned status 1 (wstat 256, 0x100)
DIED. FAILED test 1
    Failed 1/1 tests, 0.00% okay
Failed 1/1 test scripts, 0.00% okay. 1/1 subtests failed, 0.00% okay.
Failed Test Stat Wstat Total Fail  Failed  List of Failed
-------------------------------------------------------------------------
cmp_deep2.t    1   256    1    1 100.00% 1
```

The failure diagnostic shows the exact part of the data structure that failed and explains that the value Q doesn't match the regular expression $is_integer.

What about...

Q: *What if some values in the data structure may change?*

A: To ignore a specific value, use the ignore( ) function in place of the regular expression. The following example still ensures that each hash in the array has both x and y keys, but doesn't check the value of y:

```
array_each(
  {
    x => $is_integer,
    y => ignore(),
  }
);
```

Q: *What if some keys in the data structure may change?*

A: Suppose that you want to make sure that each hash contains *at least* the keys x and y. The superhashof() function ensures that the keys and values of the structure's hash appear in the given hash, but allows the given hash to contain other keys and values:

```
array_each(
  superhashof(
    {
      x => $is_integer,
      y => ignore(),
    }
  )
);
```

Similarly, Test::Deep's subhashof() function ensures that a given hash may contain some or all of the keys given in the test structure's hash, but no others.

Think of sets, supersets, and subsets.

Q: *How do I check the contents of an array when I can't predict the order of the elements?*

A: Test::Deep provides a bag() function that does exactly this. Save the following as *bag.t*:

```
use Test::More tests => 1;
use Test::Deep;

my @a - ( 4, 89, 2, 7, 1 );

cmp_deeply( \@a, bag( 1, 2, 4, 7, 89 ) );
```

Run *bag.t* to see that it passes the test. The bag() function is so common in test files that Test::Deep provides a cmp_bag() function. You can also write *bag.t* as follows:

```
use Test::More tests => 1;
use Test::Deep;

my @a = ( 4, 89, 2, 7, 1 );

cmp_bag( \@a, [ 1, 2, 4, 7, 89 ] );
```

Where to learn more

This section is only a brief overview of the Test::Deep module, which provides further comparison functions for testing objects, methods, sets (unordered arrays with unique elements), booleans, and code references. For more information, see the Test::Deep documentation.

Testing Warnings

The only parts of your code that don't need tests are those parts that you don't need. If your code produces warnings in certain circumstances and they're important to you, you need to test that they occur when and only when you expect them. The Test::Warn module provides helpful test functions to trap and examine warnings.

How do I do that?

Save the following code as *warnings.t*:

```
use Test::More tests => 4;
use Test::Warn;

sub add_positives
{
    my ( $l, $r ) = @_;
    warn "first argument ($l) was negative"  if $l < 0;
    warn "second argument ($r) was negative" if $r < 0;
    return $l + $r;
}

warning_is { is( add_positives( 8, -3 ), 5 ) }
    "second argument (-3) was negative";

warnings_are { is( add_positives( -8, -3 ), -11 ) }
    [
        'first argument (-8) was negative',
        'second argument (-3) was negative'
    ];
```

There are no commas between the first and second arguments to any of Test:: Warn's test functions because their prototypes turn normal-looking blocks into subroutine references.

Run the file with *prove* to see the following output:

```
$ prove -v warnings.t
warnings....1..4
ok 1
ok 2
ok 3
ok 4
ok
All tests successful.
Files=1, Tests=4,  0 wallclock secs ( 0.04 cusr +  0.00 csys =  0.04 CPU)
```

What just happened?

The test file declares and tests a trivial function, add_positives( ). The function adds two numbers together and warns the user if either number is less than zero.

warning_is( ) takes a block of code to run and the text of the warning expected. Like most other test functions, it takes an optional third argument as the test description. Passing two less-than-zero arguments to add_positives( ) causes the subroutine to produce two warnings. To test for multiple warnings, use Test::Warn's warnings_are( ). Instead of a single string, warnings_are( ) takes a reference to an array of complete warning strings as its second argument.

What about...

Q: *What if the warning I'm trying to match isn't an exact string?*

A: Test::Warn also exports warning_like( ), which accepts a regular expression reference instead of a complete string. Similarly, the warnings_like( ) function takes an anonymous array of regular expression references instead of just a single one. You can shorten *warnings.t* by using these functions:

```perl
use Test::More tests => 4;
use Test::Warn;

sub add_positives
{
    my ( $l, $r ) = @_;
    warn "first argument ($l) was negative"  if $l < 0;
    warn "second argument ($r) was negative" if $r < 0;
    return $l + $r;
}

warning_like { is( add_positives( 8, -3 ), 5 ) } qr/negative/;

warnings_like { is( add_positives( -8, -3 ), -11 ) }
    [ qr/first.*negative/, qr/second.*negative/ ];
```

Q: *What if I want to assert that no warnings occur in a specific block?*

A: That's a good test for when add_positives( ) adds two natural numbers. To ensure that a block of code produces no warnings, use Test::Warn's warnings_are( ) and provide an empty anonymous array:

```perl
warnings_are { is( add_positives( 4, 3 ), 7 ) } [];
```

Q: *What if I want to make sure my tests don't produce any warnings at all?*

A: Use the Test::NoWarnings module, which keeps watch for any warnings produced while the tests run. Test::NoWarnings adds an extra test at the end that ensures that no warnings have occurred.

The following listing, *nowarn.t,* tests the add_positives() function and uses Test::NoWarnings. Note that the test count has changed to accomodate the extra test:

```
use Test::More tests => 3;
use Test::NoWarnings;

sub add_positives {
    my ( $l, $r ) = @_;
    warn "first argument ($l) was negative"  if $l < 0;
    warn "second argument ($r) was negative" if $r < 0;
    return $l + $r;
}

is( add_positives( 4,  6 ), 10 );
is( add_positives( 8, -3 ),  5 );
```

The second test produces a warning, which Test::NoWarnings catches and remembers. When run, the test diagnostics show any warnings that occurred and the most recently run tests.

```
nowarn....1..3
ok 1
ok 2
not ok 3 - no warnings
#     Failed test (/usr/local/stow/perl-5.8.6/lib/5.8.6/Test/NoWarnings.
pm
               at line 45)
# There were 1 warning(s)
#         Previous test 1 ''
#         second argument (-3) was negative at nowarn.t line 7.
#   at nowarn.t line 7
#         main::add_positives(8, -3) called at nowarn.t line 12
#
# Looks like you failed 1 tests of 3.
dubious
    Test returned status 1 (wstat 256, 0x100)
DIED. FAILED test 3
    Failed 1/3 tests, 66.67% okay
Failed 1/1 test scripts, 0.00% okay. 1/3 subtests failed, 66.67% okay.
Failed Test Stat Wstat Total Fail  Failed  List of Failed
-------------------------------------------------------------------
nowarn.t       1    256     3    1  33.33%  3
```

Testing Exceptions

Sometimes things go wrong. That's okay; sometimes the best thing to do in code that detects an unrecoverable error is to pitch a fit and let higher-level code figure out what to do. If you do that, though, you need to test that behavior. As usual, there's a module to make this easy. Test:: Exception provides the functions to test that a block of code throws (or doesn't throw) the exceptions that you expect.

How do I do that?

Suppose that you're happy with add_positives() from "Testing Warnings," but your coworkers can't seem to use it correctly. They happily pass in negative numbers and ignore the warnings, and then blame you when their code fails to work properly. Your team lead has suggested that you strengthen the function to *hate* negative numbers—so much so that it throws an exception if it encounters one. How can you test that?

Save the following listing as *exception.t*:

```
use Test::More tests => 3;
use Test::Exception;
use Error;

sub add_positives
{
    my ($l, $r) = @_;
    throw Error::Simple("first argument ($l) was negative")  if $l < 0;
    throw Error::Simple("second argument ($r) was negative") if $r < 0;
    return $l + $r;
}

throws_ok { add_positives( -7,  6 ) } 'Error::Simple';
throws_ok { add_positives(  3, -9 ) } 'Error::Simple';
throws_ok { add_positives( -5, -1 ) } 'Error::Simple';
```

There are no commas between the first and second arguments to any of Test:: Exception's test functions.

Run the file with *prove*:

```
$ prove -v exception.t
exception....1..3
ok 1 - threw Error::Simple
ok 2 - threw Error::Simple
ok 3 - threw Error::Simple
ok
All tests successful.
Files=1, Tests=3,  0 wallclock secs ( 0.03 cusr +  0.00 csys =  0.03 CPU)
```

What just happened?

The call to throws_ok( ) ensures that add_positives( ) throws an exception of type Error::Simple. throws_ok( ) performs an isa( ) check on the exceptions it catches, so you can alternatively specify any superclass of the exception thrown. For example, because exceptions inherit from the Error class, you can replace all occurrences of Error::Simple in *exception.t* with Error.

What about...

Q: *How can you ensure that code doesn't throw any exceptions at all?*

A: Use Test::Exception's lives_ok( ) function.

To ensure that add_positives( ) does not throw an exception when given natural numbers, add an extra test to assert that add_positives( ) throws no exceptions:

```
use Test::More tests => 4;
use Test::Exception;
use Error;

sub add_positives
{
    my ($l, $r) = @_;
    throw Error::Simple("first argument ($l) was negative")  if $l < 0;
    throw Error::Simple("second argument ($r) was negative") if $r < 0;
    return $l + $r;
}

throws_ok { add_positives( -7,  6 ) } 'Error::Simple';
throws_ok { add_positives(  3, -9 ) } 'Error::Simple';
throws_ok { add_positives( -5, -1 ) } 'Error::Simple';
lives_ok  { add_positives(  4,  6 ) } 'no exception here!';
```

If the block throws an exception, lives_ok( ) will produce a failed test. Otherwise, the test will pass.

## CHAPTER 3

Managing Tests

All the normal rules of programming apply to tests: stay organized, reduce duplication, and don't take on more technical debt than you need. For small projects, it's easy to create and manage single test files. Large or important projects need more thought and care. Where do you put your tests? How do you organize them between files? What options do you have to reduce complexity to manageable levels?

This chapter's labs explain how to organize your test files into test suites, know and improve the reach of your tests, write your own custom testing libraries, and interpret test results.

Organizing Tests

Writing tests is easy. Managing tests well is more difficult. Having complete test coverage is worthless if running the complete test suite is so difficult that no one ever does it. Making your tests easy to run without user intervention and making it easy to interpret their results will pay off over and over again.

Using the standard testing tools that understand the Test Anything Protocol is just one part of the process. Organizing your tests sensibly is another.

How do I do that?

Consider the tests for the Test::Harness module. Download the latest distribution from the CPAN and extract it. Change into the newly created directory, run *Makefile.PL*, and build and test the module:

```
$ perl Makefile.PL
Checking if your kit is complete...
```

Look for the Download link at http://search. cpan.org/dist/ Test-Harness/.

```
Looks good
Writing Makefile for Test::Harness
$ make
cp lib/Test/Harness/TAP.pod blib/lib/Test/Harness/TAP.pod
cp lib/Test/Harness/Iterator.pm blib/lib/Test/Harness/Iterator.pm
cp lib/Test/Harness/Assert.pm blib/lib/Test/Harness/Assert.pm
cp lib/Test/Harness.pm blib/lib/Test/Harness.pm
cp lib/Test/Harness/Straps.pm blib/lib/Test/Harness/Straps.pm
cp bin/prove blib/script/prove
/usr/bin/perl5.8.6 "-MExtUtils::MY" -e "MY->fixin(shift)" blib/script/prove
<output snipped>
$ make test
PERL_DL_NONLAZY=1 /usr/bin/perl5.8.6 "-MExtUtils::Command::MM" "-e"
        "test_harness(0, 'blib/lib', 'blib/arch')" t/*.t
<output snipped>
```

What just happened?

Until now, all of the examples have mixed code and tests in the same
file. That's fine for teaching, but it won't work as well in production code.
There's no technical reason to keep all of the tests for a particular program or module in a single file, so create as many test files as you need,
organizing them by features, bugs, modules, or any other criteria.

The only technical requirement when using separate test files is that the
files must be able to load the modules they test. That means you must
manage Perl's library paths appropriately. Fortunately, most good CPAN
modules handle this. The magic of making these tests work is the magic
of Perl module installation tools such as ExtUtils::MakeMaker and
Module::Build. Test::Harness uses the former, as the presence of
Makefile.PL implies.

By convention, CPAN modules follow a standard directory hierarchy:

```
$ ls -l
total 52
drwxr-xr-x  2 chromatic wheel  4096 Jan 20 09:59 bin
-rw-r--r--  1 chromatic wheel 19110 Jan 20 09:51 Changes
drwxr-xr-x  2 chromatic wheel  4096 Jan 20 09:59 examples
drwxr-xr-x  3 chromatic wheel  4096 Jan 20 09:59 lib
-rw-r--r--  1 chromatic wheel   950 Dec 31 13:28 Makefile.PL
-rw-r--r--  1 chromatic wheel  1262 Dec 31 13:28 MANIFEST
-rw-r--r--  1 chromatic wheel   347 Jan 20 09:49 META.yml
-rw-r--r--  1 chromatic wheel   434 Dec 31 13:28 NOTES
drwxr-xr-x  4 chromatic wheel  4096 Jan 20 09:59 t
```

The -R flag causes ls to recurse into subdirectories, listing all of their files.

The modules themselves live in various subdirectories under the *lib/*
directory:

```
$ ls -1R lib/
lib:
```

```
total 4
drwxr-xr-x  3 chromatic wheel 4096 Jan 20 09:59 Test

lib/Test:
total 36
drwxr-xr-x  2 chromatic wheel  4096 Jan 20 09:59 Harness
-rw-r--r--  1 chromatic wheel 29682 Jan 20 09:35 Harness.pm

lib/Test/Harness:
total 36
-rw-r--r--  1 chromatic wheel   958 Dec 31 13:28 Assert.pm
-rw-r--r--  1 chromatic wheel  1230 Dec 31 13:28 Iterator.pm
-rw-r--r--  1 chromatic wheel 18375 Dec 31 13:28 Straps.pm
-rw-r--r--  1 chromatic wheel  5206 Dec 31 13:28 TAP.pod
```

All of the test files live under the *t/* directory:

```
$ ls -l t/
total 112
-rw-r--r--  1 chromatic wheel   541 Dec 31 13:28 00compile.t
-rw-r--r--  1 chromatic wheel   656 Dec 31 13:28 assert.t
-rw-r--r--  1 chromatic wheel   198 Dec 31 13:28 base.t
-rw-r--r--  1 chromatic wheel  2280 Dec 31 13:28 callback.t
-rw-r--r--  1 chromatic wheel   328 Dec 31 13:28 harness.t
-rw-r--r--  1 chromatic wheel   539 Dec 31 13:28 inc_taint.t
drwxr-xr-x  4 chromatic wheel  4096 Jan 20 09:59 lib
-rw-r--r--  1 chromatic wheel   151 Dec 31 13:28 nonumbers.t
-rw-r--r--  1 chromatic wheel    71 Dec 31 13:28 ok.t
-rw-r--r--  1 chromatic wheel   275 Dec 31 13:28 pod.t
-rw-r--r--  1 chromatic wheel   755 Dec 31 13:28 prove-globbing.t
-rw-r--r--  1 chromatic wheel  2143 Dec 31 13:28 prove-switches.t
drwxr-xr-x  2 chromatic wheel  4096 Jan 20 09:59 sample-tests
-rw-r--r--  1 chromatic wheel 17301 Dec 31 13:28 strap-analyze.t
-rw-r--r--  1 chromatic wheel  8913 Dec 31 13:28 strap.t
-rw-r--r--  1 chromatic wheel 26307 Dec 31 13:28 test-harness.t
```

This is output from a Unix-like system. It will look different on other platforms.

Running *Makefile.PL* or *Build.PL* (in the case of `Module::Build`) writes out either a *Makefile* or a *Build* file, respectively, that knows how to build the module and its documentation as well as how to run the tests.

The default behavior is to run everything in the *t/* directory that ends in *.t*. The full command that `make test` ran earlier shows more details:

```
PERL_DL_NONLAZY=1 /usr/bin/perl5.8.6 "-MExtUtils::Command::MM" "-e"
      "test_harness(0, 'blib/lib', 'blib/arch')" t/*.t
```

The most important part of this command is the shell pattern at the end, `t/*.t`. The shell expands it to include all of the files in the *t/* directory in sorted order.

If you've never installed this module before, how can the tests find the module files? The preceding command-line invocation includes the *blib/* subdirectories created during the make stage. Tests can also include a little magic at the beginning to set up their working environment appropriately:

```
BEGIN { chdir 't' if -d 't' }
use lib '../lib';
use blib;
```

The contents of the BEGIN block change the current directory to the *t/* directory *immediately* after Perl encounters it. This is important for the next command, which loads the lib module to add the *../lib* directory (a sibling of *t/*) to @INC. Finally, the blib module adds the *blib/lib* and *blib/arch* directories to @INC. All together, this set of commands allows you to run your tests with perl itself, not just prove, make test, or perl Build test.

As long as you follow the convention of storing modules under *lib/* and tests under *t/* and add the appropriate path manipulations to the start of the test files, you can run and distribute your tests automatically with the standard Perl tools.

What about...

Q: *How can I run tests in a specific order?*

A: Both ExtUtils::MakeMaker and Module::Build run tests in a predictable order (alphabetically, with numbers coming before names). You can control this order yourself by prepending numbers to the test names. For example, *00-first.t* will run before *99-last.t*.

If a directory full of flat files isn't enough organization for you, you can put your tests in as many subdirectories of *t/* as you like. Remember to tell your build process about the change, though! See the test attribute for *Makefile.PL* in the ExtUtils::MakeMaker documentation or the test_files parameter for *Build.PL* in the Module::Build documentation.

Q: *Do I need that magic BEGIN block? It looks complicated.*

A: Not all tests need it. It's useful if you need to know that you're in a specific directory—to create temporary files under *t/* or to load testing modules from *t/lib/*, for example. If your test file does neither, you can safely omit it.

Checking Your Coverage

Having some tests is better than having no tests, but having enough tests is better yet. *Code coverage* is one way to measure how much of the code the tests actually test. Analyzing code coverage by hand is tedious. Fortunately, the Devel::Cover module from the CPAN automates the analysis and reporting for you. Best of all, it works with the standard Perl test harness.

How do I do that?

Install Devel::Cover and its dependencies (see "Installing Test Modules" in Chapter 1). You need the ability to build XS modules, unless you install it via *ppm* or some other binary package.

From the top level of a module directory, such as Test::Harness (see "Organizing Tests," earlier in this chapter), build the module, and then run the following commands:

```
$ cover -delete
Deleting database /home/chromatic/dev/install/Test-Harness-2.46/cover_db
$ HARNESS_PERL_SWITCHES=-MDevel::Cover make test
PERL_DL_NONLAZY=1 /usr/bin/perl5.8.6 "-MExtUtils::Command::MM" "-e"
"test_harness(0, 'blib/lib', 'blib/arch')" t/*.t
t/00compile.........ok 1/5# Testing Test::Harness 2.46
t/00compile.........ok
t/assert............ok
t/base..............ok
t/callback..........ok
t/harness...........ok
t/inc_taint.........ok
t/nonumbers.........ok
t/ok................ok
t/pod...............ok
t/prove-globbing....ok
t/prove-switches....ok
t/strap-analyze.....ok
t/strap.............ok
t/test-harness......ok
        56/208 skipped: various reasons
All tests successful, 56 subtests skipped.
Files=14, Tests=551, 255 wallclock secs
    (209.59 cusr +  4.98 csys = 214.57 CPU)

$ cover
Reading database from /home/chromatic/dev/Test-Harness-2.46/cover_db
```

XS is the Perl extension system. It allows the use of code written in languages other than Perl and requires a working C development environment.

If your module uses Module::Build, use perl Build testcover instead of make test. Otherwise, install ExtUtils:: MakeMaker:: Coverage and use make testcover.

See the documentation for your shell to learn how to set the HARNESS_ PERL_ SWITCHES environment variable.

```
--------------------------------------  ------  ------  ------  ------  ------  ------
File                                      stmt  branch   cond    sub    time   total
--------------------------------------  ------  ------  ------  ------  ------  ------
blib/lib/Test/Harness.pm                  71.6   51.6    61.1   80.8    0.0    65.9
blib/lib/Test/Harness/Assert.pm          100.0  100.0    n/a   100.0    0.0   100.0
blib/lib/Test/Harness/Iterator.pm         70.0   25.0    n/a    80.0   98.9    65.5
blib/lib/Test/Harness/Straps.pm           92.9   82.7    69.0   96.2    1.0    87.6
Total                                     80.8   66.0    65.4   88.3  100.0    76.0
--------------------------------------  ------  ------  ------  ------  ------  ------
```

By default,
Devel::Cover
ignores the
coverage of any
file found in
@INC, all *.t
files, and Devel::
Cover itself. See
the +ignore,
-ignore, +inc, and
-inc options in
perldoc Devel::
Cover to learn
how to customize
this.

```
Writing HTML output to /home/chromatic/dev/Test-Harness-2.46/cover_db/
coverage.html ...
done.
```

This will take a while—several times as long as it takes your test suite to run normally. Your reward is a nice tabular summary at the end as well as some HTML files in the reported location.

What just happened?

When Devel::Cover runs a test suite, it profiles Perl code at the operational level, marking every subroutine, statement, branch, and condition in the code being tested to see if the tests actually exercise them. It writes its output to a database file from which it can produce coverage reports.

The important results are in the report shown at the end, where each file being tested has a percentage for subroutine, statement, branch, and condition coverage as well as the percentage of the time spent testing for that file and its overall coverage.

What are all of the types of coverage?

Statement coverage

Asks whether a test exercised a particular statement. Given the statement $flag = 1;, any test that causes that statement to execute will count as having covered it.

Branch coverage

Tracks whether the tests exercised both parts of a branching statement. Given the code print "True!" if $flag;, the statement must run twice—once where $flag is true and once where it is false—to achieve 100 percent branch coverage.

Condition coverage

The more complex
your conditions,
the more difficult
they are to test,
let alone read.

Considers all of the possibilities of a logical condition. Given the assignment my $name = shift || 'Ben'; within a subroutine, the test must pass in a string with an actual value for $name at least once and pass in no argument or an empty string at least once (receiving the default value) to achieve full coverage for that conditional expression.

This is a very simple type of condition coverage, with only one variable and two paths for coverage. More common are conditions with two variables: short-circuiting expressions such as $a = $x || $y have three paths for coverage, and fully evaluated expressions such as $a = $x xor $y have four paths for coverage.

Subroutine coverage

Checks that a test exercised at least part of a subroutine. If you don't have full coverage for a particular module, start with the subroutine coverage report to see which pieces of code need more tests.

Open the reports in your favorite web browser. You'll see a colorful hyperlinked summary generated by the final cover run (Figure 3-1).

Coverage Summary

Database: /home/chromatic/dev/install/Test-Harness-2.46/cover_db

file	stmt	branch	cond	sub	time	total
blib/lib/Test/Harness.pm	71.6	51.6	61.1	80.8	0.0	65.9
blib/lib/Test/Harness/Assert.pm	100.0	100.0	n/a	100.0	0.0	100.0
blib/lib/Test/Harness/Iterator.pm	70.0	25.0	n/a	80.0	98.9	65.5
blib/lib/Test/Harness/Straps.pm	92.9	82.7	69.0	96.2	1.0	87.6
Total	80.8	66.0	65.4	88.3	100.0	76.0

Figure 3-1. Coverage summary

Click on the branch, condition, or subroutine coverage links to reach a page of metrics that Devel::Cover gathered for every affected line in each tested module.

Consider the links for Test::Harness. The branch coverage is 51.6 percent. Click on that link to see a report showing line numbers for all of branches, the percentage of coverage for each branch, the true or false conditions taken for the branch, and the approximate branch expression. Figure 3-2 shows more details. The T and F columns show whether Devel::Cover believes that the tests exercised the true and false versions of the branch, respectively. A green background means yes and a red background means no. The test run of this example exercised both true and false branches of the condition in line 229, but exercised only the false branch in line 322.

Devel::Cover also runs Pod::Coverage (see "Testing Documentation Coverage," in Chapter 4) and reports its results if you have it installed.

Devel::Cover uses B::Deparse to produce the output for the branch and condition reports. This generates behaviorally—but not necessarily typographically— equivalent code.

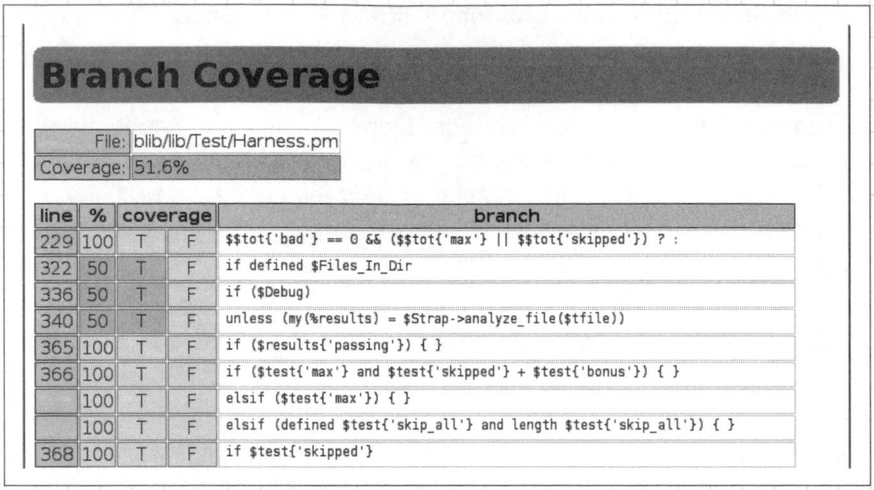

Branch Coverage

File:	blib/lib/Test/Harness.pm
Coverage:	51.6%

line	%	coverage		branch
229	100	T	F	`$$tot{'bad'} == 0 && ($$tot{'max'} || $$tot{'skipped'}) ? :`
322	50	T	F	`if defined $Files_In_Dir`
336	50	T	F	`if ($Debug)`
340	50	T	F	`unless (my(%results) = $Strap->analyze_file($tfile))`
365	100	T	F	`if ($results{'passing'}) { }`
366	100	T	F	`if ($test{'max'} and $test{'skipped'} + $test{'bonus'}) { }`
	100	T	F	`elsif ($test{'max'}) { }`
	100	T	F	`elsif (defined $test{'skip_all'} and length $test{'skip_all'}) { }`
368	100	T	F	`if $test{'skipped'}`

Figure 3-2. Branch coverage report

The condition coverage report page is more complex. For each condition, it reports the line number, the percentage of the condition the tests exercised, and the deparsed code of the conditional expression. However, the important details appear in a truth table that lists all possible boolean combinations for each element of the expression.

A is the first possible outcome of the condition, B is the second, C is the third, and so on.

In Figure 3-3, the tests exercised *none* of the possible combinations on line 210. Line 229 fared better, with the first expression tested for the two cases: where A is false and then where both A and B are true. The second expression had two tests as well, for the cases where A is false and B is true and for the case where A is true.

The final report, which shows subroutine coverage, is very simple. It lists the name and the line number of each subroutine, indicating with a red or green cell background whether the tests covered it. Figure 3-4 shows several `BEGIN` blocks (mostly `use` statements), with `strap()` and `_all_ok()` having at least some tests and `runtests()` and `_globdir()` having none.

What about...

Q: *How do I improve my test coverage?*

A: Start with the subroutine coverage report. Any subroutine marked as untested may have lurking bugs, or it may go unused throughout the code. Either way, consider the affected code carefully.

Achieving complete test coverage can be difficult; `Devel::Cover` has a complicated job to do and does it well, but it's not perfect. Running

Condition Coverage

File: blib/lib/Test/Harness.pm
Coverage: 61.1%

line	%	coverage			condition
210	0	A	B	dec	$ok xor keys %$failedtests
		0	0	0	
		0	1	1	
		1	0	1	
		1	1	0	
229	67	A	B	dec	$$tot{'bad'} == 0 && ($$tot{'max'} || $$tot{'skipped'})
		0	X	0	
		1	0	0	
		1	1	1	
	67	A	B	dec	$$tot{'max'} \|\| $$tot{'skipped'}
		0	0	0	
		0	1	1	
		1	X	1	

1 means true, 0 means false, and X means that it doesn't matter because of a short-circuited condition.

Figure 3-3. Condition coverage report

Subroutine Coverage

File: blib/lib/Test/Harness.pm
Coverage: 80.8%

line	subroutine
6	BEGIN
7	BEGIN
8	BEGIN
9	BEGIN
10	BEGIN
11	BEGIN
13	BEGIN
55	strap
201	runtests
227	_all_ok
242	_globdir

Figure 3-4. Subroutine coverage report

a recent version of Perl will help, as will upgrading to newer versions of Devel::Cover as they release. At times, you may have to simplify complex constructs or live with less than 100 percent coverage.

Perl 5.8.2 is the minimum recommended version for using Devel::Cover. Any newer version should work.

As the documentation says, though, reporting potential bugs to the *perl-qa@perl.org* mailing list is a good way to find enlightenment.

It is not always possible to achieve 100 percent coverage for all metrics. Even when it is, trying to reach that goal may not be the best use of your testing efforts. Code coverage can highlight areas in which your test suite is weak and help you reason about your code. Understand what your test suite does not test and why is valuable, even if you decide not to write a test for it.

Writing a Testing Library

By now, tests should seem less daunting. They're just programs; all of the normal good advice about design and organization applies. It makes sense to keep related code in the same place. In Perl terms, this is a module: a self-contained library of code.

Previous labs have demonstrated how to use several testing libraries. Some come with Perl's standard library. Others live on the CPAN, with new modules released frequently. If you find yourself solving the same testing problem repeatedly by twisting existing test modules in new directions, consider writing your own testing library. Test::Builder makes it possible.

How do I do that?

The use of subroutine prototypes is a convention in testing modules, but they're not like subroutine signatures in other languages. See the Prototypes section in perldoc perlsub for more information.

The following example implements one function of a very simple testing library. It adds one new function, is_between(), that tests whether a given value is between two other values. Save the code under a *lib/* directory where you can reach it (see "Installing Test Modules," in Chapter 1) as *Test/Between.pm*:

```perl
package Test::Between;

use strict;
use warnings;

use base 'Exporter';

our @EXPORT = qw( is_between );

use Test::Builder;
my $Test = Test::Builder->new();

sub is_between ($$$;$)
{
```

```
    my ($item, $lower, $upper, $desc) = @_;

    return
    (
        $Test->ok( "$lower" le "$item" && "$item" le "$upper", $desc ) ||
        $Test->diag( "          $item is not between $lower and $upper" )
    );
}

1;
```

Now you can use it within your own test programs. Save the following code as *test_between.t*:

```
#!perl

use strict;
use warnings;

use Test::More tests => 3;

use Test::Between;

is_between(    'b',  'a',  'c',  'simple alphabetical comparison' );
is_between(     2 ,   1 ,   3 ,  'simple numeric comparison'      );
is_between(  "two",   1 ,   3 ,  'mixed comparison'               );
```

Run the test with *perl*:

```
$ perl test_between.t
1..3
ok 1 - simple alphabetical comparison
ok 2 - simple numeric comparison
not ok 3 - mixed comparison
#     Failed test (examples/wtm_01.t at line 12)
#          two is not between 1 and 3
# Looks like you failed 1 test of 3.
```

What just happened?

The test file behaves just like other tests shown so far, using Test::More to set up a test plan. It also uses Test::Between just as it would any other necessary module.

Test::Between uses the Exporter module to export the is_between() function. The action starts with Test::Builder. All of the testing modules shown so far use Test::Builder internally; it provides the basic ok() function, the test plans, the test counter, and all of the output functions.

Calling Test::Builder->new() returns a singleton, the *same object every time*, to all of the testing modules. This is how it keeps the testing environment consistent.

By design, Test::Between doesn't allow its users to set the plan. Why reinvent the wheel when it's likely that users will use the module with Test:: Simple or Test:: More anyway?

Use Test::Builder and your module will work with all of the other testing modules that also use Test::Builder.

The is_between() function is simple by comparison. It has three required arguments—the value to test, the lower bound, and the upper bound—and one optional argument: the test description. The actual comparison happens on a single line:

```
"$lower" le "$item" && "$item" le "$upper"
```

This terse expression stringifies all of the arguments, then compares the lower bound to the item and the item to the upper bound. If the lower bound is less than or equal to the item and the item is less than or equal to the upper bound, the expression evaluates to true. Otherwise, it's false. Either way, the result is simple enough to pass to Test::Builder's ok() method, along with the test description.

ok() records and reports the test appropriately, returning its truth or falsehood. That allows another idiom for printing diagnostic information. If the test has failed, the return value will be false and the function will call diag() on the Test::Builder object to print the values of the item and the bounds. This makes debugging much easier, of course.

What about...

Q: *Can you add other types of comparisons?*

A: Absolutely! is_between() has a few limitations, including treating all of its arguments as strings and allowing the item to equal its lower or upper bounds. As the third test showed, it's not smart enough to know that the number the string two represents is between one and three.

Test::Between would be more useful if it allowed numeric comparisons, permitted "between but not equal" tests, and supported custom sorting routines. These are all reasonably easy additions, though: just figure out how to make the proper comparison, feed the results to $Test->ok(), report a failure diagnostic if necessary, and add the new function to @EXPORT.

Q: *How do you know that* Test::Between *works? Don't you have to write tests for your tests now?*

A: Yes, but fortunately it's not difficult. See "Testing a Testing Library," next.

Testing a Testing Library

Test::Builder makes writing custom testing libraries easy (see the previous lab, "Writing a Testing Library") by handling all of the distracting test bookkeeping and management. They're just code. Good libraries need good tests, though.

Fortunately, using Test::Builder makes writing tests for these custom libraries easier too, with a little help from Test::Builder::Tester.

How do I do that?

Consider a test suite for Test::Between (from "Writing a Testing Library"). Save the following test file as *between.t*:

```perl
#!perl

use strict;
use warnings;

use Test::Between;
use Test::Builder::Tester tests => 3;

my $desc;

$desc = 'simple alphabetical comparison';
test_pass( $desc );
is_between( 'b', 'a', 'c',  $desc );
test_test( $desc );

$desc = 'simple numeric comparison';
test_pass( $desc );
is_between(  2,  1,  3, $desc );
test_test( $desc );

$desc = 'mixed comparison';
test_out( "not ok 1 - $desc" );
test_fail( +2 );
test_diag( '        two is not between 1 and 3' );
is_between(  "two",  1,  3, $desc            );
test_test( 'failed comparison with diagnostics' );
```

The $desc variable appears multiple times so as to avoid copying and pasting the test description multiple times. Avoid repetition in tests as you would in any other code.

Run it with *perl*:

```
$ perl between.t
1..3
ok 1 - simple alphabetical comparison
ok 2 - simple numeric comparison
ok 3 - failed comparison with diagnostics
```

What just happened?

between.t looks almost like any other test that uses Test::Between except for one twist: instead of using Test::More to declare a test plan, it uses Test::Builder::Tester, which provides its own test plan. From there, it has three blocks of tests that correspond to the tests shown in "Writing a Testing Library"—an alphabetical comparison that should pass, a numeric comparison that should also pass, and a mixed comparison that should fail.

Test::Builder::Tester works by collecting information about what a test should do, running the test, and comparing its actual output to the expected output. Then it reports the results. This requires you to know if the test should pass or fail and what kind of output it will produce.

The first test should pass, so the test file calls test_pass( ) to tell Test:: Builder::Tester to expect a success message with the test description. Next, it calls the simple alphabetic comparison from the previous lab. Finally, it calls test_test( ) to compare the actual result to the expected result; this line produces the test output for Test::Harness to interpret. Passing the description here produces nicer output for humans.

Testing the numeric comparison test works the same way.

The mixed comparison test should fail, so the test file uses test_fail( ) to tell Test::Builder::Tester to expect a failure message. Because failure messages include the line number of the failing test, the sole argument to this function refers to the line number of the test call to test. That call occurs in the second line following in the test file, just after the call to test_diag( ), so the argument is +2.

Because Test::Between produces diagnostics for failed tests, the code uses test_diag( ) to test that diagnostic output.

Next comes the mixed comparison test that test_fail( ) expected, and then a test_test( ) call to compare all of the expected output—both the failure message and the diagnostics—to the received output. Test:: Builder::Tester expects the is_between( ) test to fail. If it does, the test—whether Test::Between reports failures correctly—passes.

What about...

Q: *How do you distribute tests for test modules?*

A: Either set a dependency on Test::Builder::Tester in your *Makefile. PL* or *Build.PL* file or bundle it with your code. Place it under your *t/* directory (in *t/lib/Test/Builder/Tester.pm*) and add the following lines to your test files to set its path appropriately when they run. It requires no modules outside of the standard library.

```
BEGIN
{
    chdir 't' if -d 't';
    use lib 'lib';
}
```

Q: *Debugging failed test library output is difficult. Can this be easier?*

A: `Test::Builder::Tester::Color`, which ships with `Test::Builder::Tester`, colorizes diagnostic output to make differences easier to see. It requires the `Term::ANSIColor` module, so install that too.

To enable color debugging, either add the line:

```
use Test::Builder::Tester::Color;
```

directly to your test files or load it from the command line when you run your tests:

```
$ perl -MTest::Builder::Tester::Color between.t
```

By default, matches between the received and expected output appear in green reverse type and differences appear highlighted in red reverse type.

Writing a Testing Harness

TAP is a simple protocol (see "Interpreting Test Results" in Chapter 1), but you shouldn't have to write your own parser when `Test::Harness` already knows how to interpret the results. However, `Test::Harness` only prints out what it discovers.

Test::Harness uses Test::Harness:: Straps internally.

`Test::Harness::Straps` is a thin wrapper around a TAP parser. It collects the results in a data structure but does not analyze or print them. Writing a program to report those results in an alternate format is easy. If you want to do something when tests fail, or if you want to do something more complicated than simply reporting test results, why not write your own testing harness?

How do I do that?

Save the following program somewhere in your path as *new_harness.pl* and make it executable:

```
#!perl

use strict;
use warnings;
```

```
use Test::Harness::Straps;
my $strap = Test::Harness::Straps->new( );

for my $file (@ARGV)
{
    next unless -f $file;
    my %results = $strap->analyze_file( $file );
    printf <<END_REPORT, $file, @results{qw( max seen ok skip todo bonus )};
Results for %s
    Expected tests:    %d
    Tests run:         %d
    Tested passed:     %d
    Tests skipped:     %d
    TODO tests:        %d
    TODO tests passed: %d
END_REPORT
}
```

Run it on a directory full of tests (the Test::Harness suite, for example):

Your shell should expand the file pattern t/strap*.t to include only the straps tests shown in the output.

```
$ new_harness t/strap*t
Results for t/strap-analyze.t
    Expected tests:    108
    Tests run:         108
    Tested passed:     108
    Tests skipped:     0
    TODO tests:        0
    TODO tests passed: 0
Results for t/strap.t
    Expected tests:    176
    Tests run:         176
    Tested passed:     176
    Tests skipped:     0
    TODO tests:        0
    TODO tests passed: 0
```

What just happened?

The first few lines start the program as normal, loading a few modules and pragmas and creating a new Test::Harness::Straps object. The program then loops around all filenames given on the command line, skipping them if they don't exist.

All of the magic happens in the call to analyze_file( ). This method takes the name of a test file to run, runs it, collects and parses the output, and returns a hash with details about the test file. The rest of the program prints some of these details.

As documented in Test::Harness::Straps, most of the keys of this hash are straightforward. Table 3-1 lists the most important ones.

Table 3-1. Keys of a test file's results

Key	Description
max	The number of tests planned to run
seen	The number of tests actually run
ok	The number of tests that passed
skip	The number of tests skipped
todo	The number of TODO tests encountered
bonus	The number of TODO tests that passed

Another important key is details. It contains an array reference of hashes containing details for *each* individual test. Table 3-2 explains the keys of this hash.

Table 3-2. Keys of a test's details

Key	Description
ok	Did the test pass, true or false?
actual_ok	Did it pass without being a skipped or TODO test, true or false?
name	The test description, if any.
type	The type of the test, skip, todo, or normal (an empty string).
reason	The reason for the skip or TODO, if either.

Testing Across the Network

Test::Harness::Straps makes writing custom test harnesses easy, but it's more flexible than you might think. Its input can come from *anywhere*. Have you ever wanted to run tests on a remote machine and summarize their output locally? That's no problem.

How do I do that?

Save the following code as *network_harness.pl*:

```perl
use Net::SSH::Perl;
use Test::Harness::Straps;

my $strap   = Test::Harness::Straps->new( );
my $ssh     = Net::SSH::Perl->new( 'testbox' );
$ssh->login(qw( username password ));

my ($stdout, $stderr, $exit) = $ssh->cmd( 'runtests' );
my %results = $strap->analyze_fh( 'testbox tests', $stdout );

# parse %results as normal
```

The current version of Test::Harness::Straps, as distributed with Test::Harness, is an alpha release. Andy Lester, the maintainer, plans to change the interface. Take this lab's information as a guideline and consider the module's documentation as authoritative.

The first argument to analyze_fh( ) is the test's name, corresponding to the test file name used with analyze_file( ).

Suppose that you have code running on a machine named *testbox*. You have access to that machine via SSH, and you have a program on that machine called *runtests* that knows how to run tests for your application. Run *network_harness.pl* as a normal Perl program and it will gather and parse the output from *testbox*, reporting the results.

What just happened?

The harness connects to the *testbox* machine through SSH by using the provided username and password. Then it issues the runtests command to the remote machine, collects the results, and passes the output of the command to the TAP parser object. From there, do whatever you like with the results.

What about...

Q: *Does the other machine have to have Perl running?*

A: No, it can use any other language as long as it produces TAP output.

Q: *What if you don't want to or are unable to read from a socket on the remote machine?*

A: Put the test output into an array of lines, perhaps by reading it from a web page on a remote server, and then use the analyze( ) method:

```
use LWP::Simple;
use Test::Harness::Straps;

my $strap   = Test::Harness::Straps->new( );
my $output  = get( 'http://testbox/tests/smoketest.t' );
my @lines   = split( /\n/, $output );
my %results = $strap->analyze( 'testbox smoketest', \@lines );

# parse %results as normal
```

The only trick to this example is that analyze( ) expects a reference to an array of lines of test output as its second argument. Otherwise, it behaves exactly as normal.

Automating Test Runs

Improving code quality is the primary benefit of writing a large test suite, but there are several other benefits, such as encouraging more careful coding and better design. Well-written tests provide feedback on the state of the project. At any point, anyone can run the tests to find out what works and what has broken.

This is valuable enough that, besides encouraging developers to run the test suite at every opportunity while developing, many projects automate their test suites to run unattended at regular intervals, reporting any failures. This *smoketesting* is highly valuable, as it can catch accidental mistakes as they happen, even if developers forget to run the tests on their machines or check in all of the necessary changes.

How do I do that?

Save the following code as *run_smoketest.pl*:

```perl
#!perl

use strict;
use warnings;

use constant SENDER    => 'testers@example.com';
use constant RECIPIENT => 'smoketester@example.com';
use constant MAILHOST  => 'smtp.example.com';

use Cwd;
use SVN::Client;
use Email::Send;
use Test::Harness::Straps;

my $path     = shift || die "Usage:\n$0 <repository_path>\n";
my $revision = update_repos( $path );
my $failures = run_tests(    $path );

send_report( $path, $revision, $failures );

sub update_repos
{
    my $path     = shift;
    my $ctx      = SVN::Client->new();
    return $ctx->update( $path, 'HEAD', 1 );
}

sub run_tests
{
    my $path  = shift;
    my $strap = Test::Harness::Straps->new();
    my $cwd   = cwd();

    chdir( $path );

    my @failures;

    for my $test (<t/*.t>)
    {
        my %results = $strap->analyze_file( $test );
        next if $results{passing};
```

By default, SVN:: Client uses cached credentials to log in to the Subversion repository. See its documentation to change this.

The chdir() calls exist to set up the testing environment just as if you'd run make test or perl Build test on your own.

```
                    push @failures,
                    {
                        file => $test,
                        ok   => $results{ok},
                        max  => $results{max},
                    };
                }

                chdir( $cwd );

                return \@failures;
        }

        sub send_report
        {
                my ($revision, $path, $failures) = @_;
                return unless @$failures;

                my $message = sprintf(<<END_HEADER, RECIPIENT, SENDER,
                    $path, $revision);
To: %s
From: %s
Subect: Failed Smoketest For %s at Revision %d

END_HEADER

                for my $failure (@$failures)
                {
                        $message .= sprintf( "%s:\n\tExpected: %d\n\tPassed: %d\n",
                            @$failure{qw( file max ok )} );
                }

                send( 'SMTP', $message, MAILHOST );
        }
```

Be sure to install a recent version of Test::Harness, Email::Send, and Subversion with its Perl bindings. Modify the three constants at the top of the file to reflect your network setup.

Run the program, passing it the path to the working version directory of a Subversion repository. For example:

```
$ perl run_smoketest.pl ~/dev/repos/Text-WikiFormat/trunk
```

If any of the tests fail, you'll receive an email report about the failures:

```
To: smoketest@example.com
From: smoketest_bot@example.com
Subect: Failed Smoketest at Revision 19

t/fail.t:
    Expected: 3
    Passed: 2
```

If you receive svn_path_join errors, remove the trailing slash from the working directory path.

What just happened?

run_smoketest.pl is three programs at once, with a little bit of glue. First, it's a very simple Subversion client, thanks to the SVN::Client module. Second, it's a test harness, thanks to Test::Harness::Straps (see "Writing a Testing Harness," earlier in this chapter). Third, it's an email reporter, using Email::Send.

The program starts by pulling in the path to an existing Subversion repository. It then calls update_repos() which creates a new SVN::Client module and updates the repository with the absolute freshest code (denoted by the symbolic constant HEAD tag in CVS and Subversion), recursively updating all directories beneath it. It returns the number of this revision.

Next, run_tests() cycles through each file with the *.t* extension in the the repository's *t/* directory. It collects the results of only the failed tests—those for which the passing key is false—and returns them in an array.

The program then calls send_report() to notify the recipient address about the failures. If there are none, the function returns. Otherwise, it builds up a simple email, reporting each failed test with its name and the number of expected and passing tests. Finally, it sends the message to the specified address, where developers and testers can pore over the results and fix the failures.

Many other revision control systems have Perl bindings, but you can also use their command-line tools directly from your programs.

What about...

Q: *How do you run only specific tests? What if you have benchmarks and other long-running tests in a different directory?*

A: Customize the glob pattern in the loop in run_tests() to focus on as many or as few tests as you like.

Q: *Is it possible to automate the smoketest?*

A: Because *run_smoketest.pl* takes the repository path on the command line, it can run easily from cron. Beware, though, that Test::Harness::Straps 2.46 and earlier spit out diagnostic information to STDERR. You may need to redirect this to */dev/null* or the equivalent to avoid sending messages to yourself.

Q: *Could the report include other details, such as the diagnostics of each failed test?*

A: The limitation here is in what Test::Harness::Straps provides. Keep watching future releases for more information.

The Aegis software configuration management system (http://aegis.sourceforge.net/) takes this idea further, requiring all check-ins to include tests that fail before the modifications and that pass after them.

Q: *CVS and Subversion both provide ways to run programs when a developer checks in a change. Can this smoketest run then?*

A: Absolutely! This is an excellent way to ensure that no one can make changes that break the main branch.

## CHAPTER 4

Distributing Your Tests (and Code)

The goal of all testing is to improve the quality of code. Quality isn't just the absence of bugs and features behaving as intended. High-quality code and projects install well, behave well, have good and useful documentation, and demonstrate reliability and care outside of the code itself. If your users can run the tests too, that's a good sign.

It's not always easy to build quality into a system, but if you can test your project, you can improve its quality. Perl has several tools and techniques to distribute tests and test the non-code portions of your projects. The labs in this chapter demonstrate how to use them and what they can do for you.

Testing POD Files

The Plain Old Documentation format, or POD, is the standard for Perl documentation. Every Perl module distribution should contain some form of POD, whether in standalone *.pod* files or embedded in the modules and programs themselves.

As you edit documentation in a project, you run the risk of making errors. While typos and omissions can be annoying and distracting, formatting errors can render your documentation incorrectly or even make it unusable. Missing an =cut on inline POD may cause bizarre failures by turning working code into documentation. Fortunately, a test suite can check the syntax of all of the POD in your distribution.

How do I do that?

Consider a module distribution for a popular racing sport. The directory structure contains a *t/* directory for the tests and a *lib/* directory for the modules and POD documents. To test all of the POD in a distribution, create an extra test file, *t/pod.t*, as follows:

```
use Test::More;

eval 'use Test::Pod 1.00';
plan( skip_all => 'Test::Pod 1.00 required for testing POD' ) if $@;

all_pod_files_ok();
```

Run the test file with *prove*:

```
$ prove -v t/pod.t
t/pod....1..3
ok 1 - lib/Sports/NASCAR/Car.pm
ok 2 - lib/Sports/NASCAR/Driver.pm
ok 3 - lib/Sports/NASCAR/Team.pm
ok
All tests successful.
Files=1, Tests=3,  0 wallclock secs ( 0.45 cusr +  0.03 csys =  0.48 CPU)
```

What just happened?

People who build modules likely need to run the tests. People who install prebuilt packages may not.

Because Test::Pod is a prerequisite only for testing, it's an optional prerequisite for the distribution. The second and third lines of *t/pod.t* check to see whether the user has Test::Pod installed. If not, the test file skips the POD-checking tests.

One of the test functions exported by Test::Pod is all_pod_files_ok( ). If given no arguments, it finds all Perl-related files in a *blib/* or *lib/* directory within the current directory. It declares a plan, planning one test per file found. The previous example finds three files, all of which have valid POD.

If Test::Pod finds a file that doesn't contain any POD at all, the test for that file will be a success.

What about...

Q: *How can I test a specific list of files?*

A: Pass all_pod_files_ok( ) an array of filenames of all the files to check. For example, to test the three files that Test::Pod found previously, change *t/pod.t* to:

```
use Test::More;

eval 'use Test::Pod 1.00';
plan( skip_all => 'Test::Pod 1.00 required for testing POD' ) if $@;
```

```
all_pod_files_ok(
    'lib/Sports/NASCAR/Car.pm',
    'lib/Sports/NASCAR/Driver.pm',
    'lib/Sports/NASCAR/Team.pm'
);
```

Q: *Should I ship POD-checking tests with my distribution?*

A: There's no strong consensus in the Perl QA community one way or the other, except that it's valuable for developers to run these tests before releasing a new version of the project. If the POD won't change as part of the build process, asking users to run the tests may have little practical value besides demonstrating that you consider the validity of your documentation to be important.

For projects released to the CPAN, the CPAN Testing Service (*http://cpants.dev.zsi.at/*) currently considers the presence of POD-checking tests as a mark of "kwalitee" (see "Validating Kwalitee," later in this chapter). Not everyone agrees with this metric.

Testing Documentation Coverage

When defining an API, every function or method should have some documentation explaining its purpose. That's a good goal—one worth capturing in tests. Without requiring you to hardcode the name of every documented function, Test::Pod::Coverage can help you to ensure that all the subroutines you expect other people to use have proper POD documentation.

How do I do that?

Assume that you have a module distribution for a popular auto-racing sport. The distribution's base directory contains a *t/* directory with tests and a *lib/* directory with modules. Create a test file, *t/pod-coverage.t*, that contains the following:

```
use Test::More;

eval 'use Test::Pod::Coverage 1.04';
plan(
    skip_all => 'Test::Pod::Coverage 1.04 required for testing POD coverage'
) if $@;

all_pod_coverage_ok();
```

Module::Starter creates a pod-coverage.t test file if you use it to create the framework for your distribution.

Run the test file with *prove* to see output similar to:

```
$ prove -v t/pod-coverage.t
t/pod-coverage....1..3
not ok 1 - Pod coverage on Sports::NASCAR::Car
```

```
#     Failed test (/usr/local/share/perl/5.8.4/Test/Pod/Coverage.pm
            at line 112)
# Coverage for Sports::NASCAR::Car is 75.0%, with 1 naked subroutine:
#       restrictor_plate
ok 2 - Pod coverage on Sports::NASCAR::Driver
ok 3 - Pod coverage on Sports::NASCAR::Team
# Looks like you failed 1 tests of 3.
dubious
        Test returned status 1 (wstat 256, 0x100)
DIED. FAILED test 1
        Failed 1/3 tests, 66.67% okay
Failed Test     Stat Wstat Total Fail  Failed  List of Failed
-------------------------------------------------------------------------
t/pod-coverage.t   1   256     3    1  33.33%  1
Failed 1/1 test scripts, 0.00% okay. 1/3 subtests failed, 66.67% okay.
```

What just happened?

The test file starts as normal, setting up paths to load the modules to test. The second and third lines of *t/pod-coverage.t* check to see whether the Test::Pod::Coverage module is available. If is isn't, the tests cannot continue and the test exits.

Test::Pod::Coverage exports the all_pod_coverage_ok() function, which finds all available modules and tests their POD coverage. It looks for a *lib/* or *blib/* directory in the current directory and plans one test for each module that it finds.

Unfortunately, the output of the *prove* command reveals that there's some work to do: the module Sports::NASCAR::Car is missing some documentation for a subroutine called restrictor_plate(). Further investigation of *lib/Sports/NASCAR/Car.pm* reveals that documentation is lacking indeed:

```
=head2 make

Returns the make of this car, e.g., "Dodge".

=cut

sub make
{
    ...
}

sub restrictor_plate
{
    ...
}
```

In the previous listing, make() has documentation, but restrictor_plate() has none.

Pod::Coverage considers a subroutine to have documentation if there exists an =head or =item that describes it somewhere in the module. The restrictor_plate() subroutine clearly lacks either of these. Add the following to satisfy that heuristic:

```
=head2 make

Returns the make of this car, e.g., "Dodge".

=cut

sub make
{
    ...
}

=head2 restrictor_plate

Returns whether this car has a restrictor plate installed.

=cut

sub restrictor_plate
{
    ...
}
```

Run the test again to see it pass:

```
$ prove -v t/pod-coverage.t
t/pod-coverage....1..3
ok 1 - Pod coverage on Sports::NASCAR::Car
ok 2 - Pod coverage on Sports::NASCAR::Driver
ok 3 - Pod coverage on Sports::NASCAR::Team
ok
All tests successful.
Files=1, Tests=3,  1 wallclock secs ( 0.51 cusr +  0.03 csys -  0.54 CPU)
```

What about...

Q: *I have private functions that I don't want to document, but* Test::Pod::Coverage *complains that they don't have documentation. How can I fix that?*

A: See the Test::Pod::Coverage documentation for the also_private and trustme parameters. These come from Pod::Coverage, which also has good documentation well worth reading. By default, Test::Pod::Coverage makes some smart assumptions that functions beginning with underscores and functions with names in all caps are private.

Distribution Signatures

Cryptographically signing a distribution is more of an integrity check than a security measure. As the documentation for Test::Signature explains, by the time the make test portion of the installation checks the signature of a module, you've already executed a *Makefile.PL* or *Build.PL*, giving potentially malicious code the chance to run. Still, a signed distribution assures you that every file in the distribution is exactly what the author originally uploaded.

Signing a module distribution creates a file called *SIGNATURE* in the top-level directory that contains checksums for every file in the distribution. The author then signs the *SIGNATURE* file with a PGP or equivalent key. If you sign your distribution, you should include a signature validity check as part of the test suite.

How do I do that?

To sign a module, first install GnuPG and set up a private key that you'll use to do the signing with. For more information on how to use GnuPG, see the Documentation section on the GnuPG web site at *http://www. gnupg.org/*.

Next, install Module::Signature. Module::Signature provides the cpansign utility to create and verify *SIGNATURE* files. Describing module signatures, how to use cpansign, and considerations when bundling up modules is a bigger topic than this lab allows, so please see the Module:: Signature documentation for information on how to sign your modules.

Once you've signed your distribution, you should see a *SIGNATURE* file in the distribution's directory containing something like:

```
This file contains message digests of all files listed in MANIFEST,
signed via the Module::Signature module, version 0.44.
...
-----BEGIN PGP SIGNED MESSAGE-----
Hash: SHA1

SHA1 e72320c0cd1a851238273f7d1jd7d46t395mrjbs Changes
SHA1 fm8b86bb3d933345751371f67chd01efe8tdua9f3 MANIFEST
SHA1 67i17fa0ff0ea897b0a2e43ddac01m6e5r8n132s META.yml
SHA1 cc0l0c8abd8a9941b1y0ad61fr808i7hfbcc32al Makefile.PL
SHA1 1fa0y76d5dac6c64d15lb17f0td22l1sfmau2cci README
SHA1 fd94a423d3e42462fec2if7997a19y8b6abs3f7m lib/FAQ/Sciuridae.pm
SHA1 b7504edf3808b62742e3bm00dc464d3i9lf2b39m lib/FAQ/Sciuridae/Chipmunk.pm
SHA1 edde6f2c4608bfeee6acf9effff9644jbc815d6e lib/FAQ/Sciuridae/Marmot.pm
...
```

To verify the contents of *SIGNATURE* when the test suite is run, create a test file *00-signature.t*:

```
use Test::More;

eval 'use Test::Signature';

plan( skip_all => 'Test::Signature required for signature verification' )
    if $@;
plan( tests => 1 );
signature_ok();
```

Run the test file with *prove*:

```
$ prove -v t/00-signature.t
t/00-signature....1..1
ok 1 - Valid signature
ok
All tests successful.
Files=1, Tests=1,  1 wallclock secs ( 0.57 cusr +  0.05 csys =  0.62 CPU)
```

Because a broken signature is a showstopper when installing modules, it is common practice to prefix the file name with zeroes so that it runs early in the test suite.

What just happened?

Validating signatures is only a suggested step in installing modules, not a required one. Thus, *00-signature.t* checks to see whether the user has Module::Signature installed. It skips signature verification if not.

By default, Test::Signature exports a single function, signature_ok(), which reports a single test that indicates the validity of the *SIGNATURE* file.

To verify a *SIGNATURE* file, the test first checks the integrity of the PGP signature contained within. Next, it creates a list of checksums for the files listed in *MANIFEST*, comparing that list to the checksums supplied in *SIGNATURE*. If all of these steps succeed, the test produced by signature_ok() succeeds.

Internally, Test::Signature's signature_ok() function and running cpansign -v use the same verify() function found in Module::Signature. If one of the steps to test the integrity of *SIGNATURE* fails, signature_ok() will produce the same or similar output to that of cpansign -v. For example, if one or more of the checksums is incorrect, the output will display a comparison of the list of checksums in the style of the *diff* utility.

Testing Entire Distributions

A proper Perl distribution contains a handful of files and lists any prerequisite modules that it needs to function properly. Each package should have a version number and have valid POD syntax. If you've signed your distribution cryptographically, the signature should validate. These are all important features, so why not test them?

The Test::Distribution module can do just that with one simple test script.

How do I do that?

Given a module distribution Text::Hogwash, create a test file *t/distribution.t* containing:

```
use Test::More;

eval 'require Test::Distribution';
plan( skip_all => 'Test::Distribution not installed' ) if $@;
Test::Distribution->import();
```

The -l option tells *prove* that modules for the distribution are in the *lib/* directory. Run *t/distribution.t* using *prove*:

```
$ prove -v -l t/distribution.t
t/distribution....1..14
ok 1 - Checking MANIFEST integrity
ok 2 - use Text::Hogwash::Tomfoolery;
ok 3 - use Text::Hogwash::Silliness;
ok 4 - Text::Hogwash::Tomfoolery defines a version
ok 5 - Text::Hogwash::Silliness defines a version
ok 6 - All non-core use()d modules listed in PREREQ_PM
ok 7 - POD test for lib/Text/Hogwash/Tomfoolery.pm
ok 8 - POD test for lib/Text/Hogwash/Silliness.pm
ok 9 - MANIFEST exists
ok 10 - README exists
ok 11 - Changes or ChangeLog exists
ok 12 - Build.PL or Makefile.PL exists
ok 13 - Pod Coverage ok
ok 14 - Pod Coverage ok
ok
All tests successful.
Files=1, Tests=14,  0 wallclock secs ( 0.19 cusr +  0.01 csys =  0.20 CPU)
```

What just happened?

Test::Distribution calculates how many tests it will run and declares the plan during its import() call. Some of these tests use modules covered earlier, such as Test::Pod ("Testing POD Files"), Test::Pod::Coverage ("Testing Documentation Coverage"), and Module::Signature ("Distribution Signatures"). Others are simple checks that would be tedious to perform manually, such as ensuring that the *MANIFEST* and *README* files exist.

What about...

Q: *Is it possible to test a subset of distribution properties, such as the module prerequisites or package versions?*

A: The Test::Distribution documentation includes a list of the types of tests it performs, such as prereq and versions. Specify the types of tests you want to run by using only or not after the import statement:

```
Test::Distribution->import( only => [ qw( prereq versions ) ] );
```

The previous listing passes two additional arguments to import( ): the string only and a reference to an array of the strings that represent the only types of tests that Test::Distribution should perform. When running the modified test file, the test output is much shorter because Test::Distribution runs only the named tests:

```
$ prove -v t/distribution.t
t/distribution....1..5
ok 1 - use Text::Hogwash::Tomfoolery;
ok 2 - use Text::Hogwash::Silliness;
ok 3 - Text::Hogwash::Tomfoolery defines a version
ok 4 - Text::Hogwash::Silliness defines a version
ok 5 - All non-core use( )d modules listed in PREREQ_PM
ok
All tests successful.
Files=1, Tests=5,  1 wallclock secs ( 0.62 cusr +  0.04 csys =  0.66
CPU)
```

You can also use the not argument instead of only to prohibit Test::Distribution from running specified tests. It will run everything else.

Letting the User Decide

Installing a Perl module distribution is not always as simple as running the build file and testing and installing it. Some modules present the user with configuration options, such as whether to include extra features or to install related utilities. The example tests shown previously have simply skipped certain tests when prerequisite modules are not present. In other cases, it is appropriate to ask the user to decide to run or to skip tests that require network connectivity or tests that may take an exorbitant amount of time to finish.

For example, consider the hypothetical module MD5::Solve, which reverses one-way MD5 checksums at the cost of an incredible amount of time, not to mention computing power and practicality. Performing this sort of task for even a small amount of data is costly, and the test suite for this module must take even more time to run. When installing the module, the user should have the option of skipping the expensive tests.

How do I do that?

ExtUtils::MakeMaker and Module::Build provide prompt() functions that prompt and receive input from the user who is installing the module. The functions take one or two arguments: a message to display to the user and a default value. These functions check the environment to make sure a human is indeed sitting at the terminal and, if so, display the message and wait for the user to enter a string. If there is no user present—in the case of an automated install, for example—they return the default value.

Using ExtUtils::MakeMaker, the build script for the module *Makefile.PL*, appears as follows:

```perl
use strict;
use warnings;
use ExtUtils::MakeMaker qw( WriteMakefile prompt );

my %config = (
    NAME          => 'MD5::Solve',
    AUTHOR        => 'Emily Anne Perlmonger <emmils@example.com>',
    VERSION_FROM  => 'lib/MD5/Solve.pm',
    ABSTRACT_FROM => 'lib/MD5/Solve.pm',
    PREREQ_PM     => { 'Test::More' => 0, },
    dist          => { COMPRESS => 'gzip -9f', SUFFIX => 'gz', },
    clean => { FILES => 'MD5-Solve-*' },
);

my @patterns = qw( t/*.t );

print "==> Running the extended test suite may take weeks or years! <==\n";
my $answer = prompt( 'Do you want to run the extended test suite?', 'no' );

if ( $answer =~ m/^y/i )
{
    print "I'm going to run the extended tests.\n";
    push @patterns, 't/long/*.t';
}
```

```
    else
    {
        print "Skipping extended tests.\n";
    }

    $config{test} = { TESTS => join ' ', map { glob } @patterns };

    WriteMakefile(%config);
```

Running the build script generates a *Makefile* and displays the following output, prompting the user to make a decision:

```
$ perl Makefile.PL
==> Running the extended test suite may take weeks or years! <==
Do you want to run the extended test suite? [no] no
Skipping extended tests.
Checking if your kit is complete...
Looks good
Writing Makefile for MD5::Solve
```

What just happened?

Many *Makefile.PL* files consist of a single `WriteMakefile()` statement. The previous *Makefile.PL* has an additional bit of logic to determine which sets of test scripts to run. The test files in *t/* always run, but those in *t/long/* run only if the user consents.

This file stores all of the options that a typical *Makefile.PL* provides to `WriteMakefile()` in a hash instead. By default, the program expands the pattern `t/*.t` into filenames that use `glob` by using the techniques described in "Bundling Tests with Modules," later in this chapter. The program then adds these filenames to %config.

Before modifying %config, however, the file uses the `prompt()` function to ask the user to decide whether to run the lengthy tests. If the user's answer begins with the letter y, the code adds the glob string `t/long/*.t` to the list of patterns of test files to run as part of the test suite during make test:

```
$ make test
cp lib/MD5/Solve.pm blib/lib/MD5/Solve.pm
PERL_DL_NONLAZY=1 /usr/bin/perl "-MExtUtils::Command::MM" "-e"
    "test_harness(0, 'blib/lib', 'blib/arch')" t/00.load.t t/pod-coverage.t
    t/pod.t t/long/alphanumeric.t t/long/digits.t t/long/long-string.t
    t/long/longer-string.t t/long/punctuation.t t/long/random.t
    t/long/short.t t/long/simple.t
t/00.load...............ok
t/long/alphanumeric.....ok
t/long/digits...........ok
t/long/long-string......ok
t/long/longer-string....ok
```

```
t/long/punctuation......ok
t/long/random...........ok
...
```

However, if ExtUtils::MakeMaker decides not to ask for user input or the user hits the Enter key to accept the default value, the return value of prompt() will be no. In the previous example, the user entered no explicitly, so the tests in *t/long/* will not run:

```
$ make test
cp lib/MD5/Solve.pm blib/lib/MD5/Solve.pm
PERL_DL_NONLAZY=1 /usr/bin/perl "-MExtUtils::Command::MM" "-e"
    "test_harness(0, 'blib/lib', 'blib/arch')" t/00.load.t t/pod-coverage.t
    t/pod.t
t/00.load.........ok
t/pod-coverage....ok
t/pod.............ok
All tests successful.
Files=3, Tests=3,  1 wallclock secs ( 1.09 cusr +  0.09 csys =  1.18 CPU)
```

Letting the User Decide (Continued)

Module::Build provides a prompt() method that takes the same arguments as the prompt() function exported by ExtUtils::MakeMaker. However, this prompt() is a method, so either call it on the Module::Build class or a Module::Build or subclass object.

Module::Build also provides a y_n() method that returns either true or false, to simplify asking boolean questions. The y_n() method takes the same arguments as prompt(), except that the default answer, if supplied, must be either y or n.

How do I do that?

The *Build.PL* file for the MD5::Solve module is:

```
use strict;
use warnings;
use Module::Build;

print "==> Running the extended test suite may take weeks or years! <==\n";
my $answer = Module::Build->y_n(
    'Do you want to run the extended test suite?', 'n'
);

my $patterns = 't/*.t';

if ($answer)
{
```

```
        print "I'm going to run the extended tests.\n";
        $patterns .= ' t/long/*.t';
    }
    else
    {
        print "Skipping extended tests.\n";
    }

    my $builder = Module::Build->new(
        module_name        => 'MD5::Solve',
        license            => 'perl',
        dist_author        => 'Emily Anne Perlmonger <emmils@cxample.com>',
        dist_version_from  => 'lib/MD5/Solve.pm',
        build_requires     => { 'Test::More' => 0, },
        add_to_cleanup     => ['MD5-Solve-*'],
        test_files         => $patterns,
    );

    $builder->create_build_script();
```

Module::Build automatically expands the pattern(s) of files given to test_files.

Run *Build.PL* to see:

```
$ perl Build.PL
==> Running the extended test suite may take weeks or years! <==
Do you want to run the extended test suite? [n] n
Skipping extended tests.
Checking whether your kit is complete...
Looks good
Creating new 'Build' script for 'MD5-Solve' version '0.01'
```

What just happened?

Similar to the Makefile.PL example earlier, the build script prompts the user whether to run the extended tests. If the user responds positively, $answer will be true, and the code will append t/long/*.t to the list of patterns of files to run in the test suite. Otherwise, only test files matching t/*.t will run during make test.

Bundling Tests with Modules

When releasing modules, you should always include a test suite so that the people installing your code can have confidence that it works on their systems. Tools such as the CPAN shell will refuse to install a distribution if any of its tests fail, unless the user forces a manual installation. If you upload the module to the CPAN, a group of dedicated individuals will report the results of running your test suite on myriad platforms. The CPAN Testers site at *http://testers.cpan.org/* reports their results.

This lab explains how to set up a basic distribution, including the directory structure and minimal test suite.

How do I do that?

Module distributions are archives that, when extracted, produce a standard directory tree. Every distribution should contain at least a *lib/* directory for the reusable module files, a *Build.PL* or *Makefile.PL* to aid in testing and installing the code, and a *t/* directory that contains the tests for the module and any additional data needed for testing.

If you haven't already created a directory structure for the distribution, the simplest way to start is by using the `module-starter` command from the `Module::Starter` distribution. `module-starter` creates the directories you need and even includes sample tests for your module.

Go ahead and install `Module::Starter`. Once installed, you should also have the `module-starter` program in your path. Create a fictitious distribution for calculating taxes that includes two modules, `Taxes::Autocomplete` and `Taxes::Loophole`:

Perl's documentation suggests using h2xs to create new modules. Module::Starter is just a modern alternative.

```
$ module-starter --mb --distro=Taxes \
    --module=Taxes::Autocomplete,Taxes::Loophole
    --author='John Q. Taxpayer' \
    --email='john@bigpockets.com' --verbose
Created Taxes
Created Taxes/lib/Taxes
Created Taxes/lib/Taxes/Autocomplete.pm
Created Taxes/lib/Taxes/Loophole.pm
Created Taxes/t
Created Taxes/t/pod-coverage.t
Created Taxes/t/pod.t
Created Taxes/t/00-load.t
Created Taxes/Build.PL
Created Taxes/MANIFEST
Created starter directories and files
```

`module-starter` creates a complete distribution in the directory *Taxes/*. Further inspection of the *Taxes/t/* directory reveals three test files:

```
$ ls -1 Taxes/t/
00-load.t
pod-coverage.t
pod.t
```

Any test files you add to *Taxes/t/* will run during the testing part of the module installation.

What just happened?

The `module-starter` command creates a skeleton directory structure for new modules. This structure includes the three test files in the previous output. These files perform basic tests to make sure your module maintains a certain level of quality (or "kwalitee"—see "Validating Kwali-tee," later in this chapter).

t/pod-coverage.t and *t/pod.t* test POD documentation validity and cover-age, respectively. *t/00-load.t* contains the "basic usage" test, which may be the most common type of test within different Perl module distribu-tions. This test simply checks whether the modules in the distribution load properly. Note that module-starter has lovingly filled in all of the module names for you:

```
use Test::More tests => 2;

BEGIN
{
    use_ok( 'Taxes::Autocomplete' );
    use_ok( 'Taxes::Loophole' );
}

diag( "Testing Taxes::Autocomplete $Taxes::Autocomplete::VERSION,
        Perl 5.008004, /usr/bin/perl" ),
```

You might see the same sort of tests in a test file with a different name, such as *00_basic.t* or just *load.t*, or it may be one of several tests in another file.

What about?

Q: *I have 8,000 test files in my t/ directory! Can I use subdirectories to organize them better?*

A: Sure thing. If you use Module::Build, specify a test_files key whose value is a space-delimited string containing just the patterns of test files. Module::Build automatically expands the patterns.

```
use Module::Build;

my $build = Module::Build->new(
    ...
        test_files => 't/*.t t/*/*.t',
    ...
);

$builder->create_build_script();
```

Alternatively, set the recursive_test_files flag to use every *.t* file found within the *t/* directory and all of its subdirectories:

```
use Module::Build;

my $build = Module::Build->new(
    ...
        recursive_test_files => 1,
```

```
    ...
);

$builder->create_build_script();
```

If you use ExtUtils::MakeMaker and *Makefile.PL* instead, do the equivalent by providing a test key to the hash given to WriteMakefile():

```
use ExtUtils::MakeMaker;

WriteMakeFile(
    ...
    test => { TESTS => join ' ', map { glob } qw( t/*.t t/*/*.t ) },
    ...
);
```

The value of the test hash pair must be a hash reference with the key TESTS. The value is a space-delimited string of all test files to run. In the previous example, join and glob create such a a string based on the two patterns t/*.t and t/*/*.t. This is necessary because WriteMakeFile() will not automatically expand the patterns when used with ActiveState Perl on Windows.

Collecting Test Results

Distributing your tests with your code is a good diagnostic practice that can help you to ensure that your code works when your users try to run it. At least it's good for diagnostics when you can convince your users to send you the appropriate test output. Rather than walk them through the steps of running the tests, redirecting their output to files, and sending you the results, consider automating the process of gathering failed test output and useful information.

As usual, the CPAN has the solution in the form of Module::Build:: TestReporter.

How do I do that?

Consider a Chef module that can slice, dice, fricassee, and boil ingredients. Create a new directory for it, with *lib/* and *t/* subdirectories. Save the following code as *lib/Chef.pm*:

```
package Chef;

use base 'Exporter';

use strict;
use warnings;
```

```perl
our $VERSION = '1.0';
our @EXPORT  = qw( slice dice fricassee );

sub slice
{
    my $ingredient = shift;
    print "Slicing $ingredient...\n";
}

sub dice
{
    my $ingredient = shift;
    print "Dicing $ingredient...\n";
}

sub fricassee
{
    my $ingredient = shift;
    print "Fricasseeing $ingredient...\n";
}

sub boil
{
    my $ingredient = shift;
    print "Boiling $ingredient...\n";
}

1;
```

Yes, the missing export of boil ( ) is intentional.

Save a basic, "does it compile?" test file as *t/use.t*:

```perl
#!perl

use strict;
use warnings;

use Test::More tests => 1;

my $module  = 'Chef';
use_ok( $module ) or exit;
```

Save the following test of its exports as *t/chef_exports.t*:

```perl
#!perl

use strict;
use warnings;

use Test::More tests => 5;

my $module  = 'Chef';
use_ok( $module ) or exit;

for my $export (qw( slice dice fricassee boil ))
{
    can_ok( __PACKAGE__, $export );
}
```

Finally, save the following build file as *Build.PL*:

```
use Module::Build::TestReporter;

my $build = Module::Build::TestReporter->new(
        module_name      => 'Chef',
        license          => 'perl',
        report_file      => 'chef_failures.txt',
        report_address   => 'chef-failures@example.com',
        dist_version_from => 'lib/Chef.pm',
);

$build->create_build_script();
```

Now build the module as normal and run the tests:

```
$ perl Build.PL
Creating new 'Build' script for 'Chef' version '1.0'
$ perl Build
lib/Chef.pm -> blib/lib/Chef.pm
$ perl Build test
t/use.t...ok
Tests failed!
Please e-mail 'chef_failures.txt' to chef-failures@example.com.
```

What just happened?

Hang on, that's a lot different from normal. What's *chef_failures.txt*? Open it with a text editor; it contains output from the failed tests as well as information about the currently running Perl binary:

```
Test failures in 't/chef.t' (1/5):
5: - main->can('boil')
            Failed test (t/chef.t at line 13)
   main->can('boil') failed

Summary of my perl5 (revision 5 version 8 subversion 6) configuration:
<...>
```

Module::Build::TestReporter diverts the output of the test run and reports any failures to the file specified in *Build.PL*'s report_file parameter. It also prints a message about the failures and gives the address to which to send the results.

What happens if the tests all succeed? Open *lib/Chef.pm* and change the export line:

```
@EXPORT  = qw( slice dice fricassee boil );
```

Then run the tests again:

```
$ perl Build test
All tests passed.
```

You're happy, the users are happy, and there's nothing left to do.

This lowers the barrier for users to report test failures. You don't have to walk them through running the tests in verbose mode, trying to capture the output. All they have to do is to email you the report file.

What about...

Q: *What if I already have a* Module::Build *subclass?*

A: Make your subclass inherit from Module::Build::TestReporter instead. See the module's documentation for other ideas, too!

Q: *Can I have* Module::Build::TestReporter *email me directly? How about if it posted the results to a web page? That would make it even easier to retrieve failure reports from users.*

A: It would, but can you guarantee that everyone running your tests has a working Internet connection or an SMTP server configured for Perl to use? If so, feel free to subclass Module::Build::TestReporter to report directly to you.

Q: *My output looks different. Why?*

A: This lab covered an early version of the module. It may change its messages slightly. The basic functions will remain the same, though. As with all of the other testing modules, see the documentation for current information.

Validating Kwalitee

After all of the work coming up with the idea for your code, writing your code, and testing your code (or writing the tests and then writing the code), you may be ready to share your masterpiece with the world. You may feel understandably nervous; even though you know you have good tests, many other things could go wrong—things you won't recognize until they do go wrong.

Fortunately, the Perl QA group has put together loose guidelines of code kwalitee based on hard-won experience about what makes installing and using software easy and what makes it difficult. The CPAN Testing Service, or CPANTS, currently defines code kwalitee in 17 ways; see *http://cpants. dev.zsi.at/kwalitee.html* for more information.

Rather than walking through all 17 indicators by hand, why not automate the task?

How do I do that?

Download and install Test::Kwalitee. Then add the following code to your *t/* directory as *kwalitee.t*:

```
#!perl

eval { require Test::Kwalitee };
exit if $@;
Test::Kwalitee->import();
```

Then run the code with *perl*:

```
$ perl t/kwalitee.t
1..8
ok 1 - checking permissions
ok 2 - looking for symlinks
ok 3 - needs a Build.PL or Makefile.PL
ok 4 - needs a MANIFEST
ok 5 - needs a META.yml
ok 6 - needs a README
ok 7 - POD should have no errors
ok 8 - code should declare all non-core prereqs
```

What just happened?

The test file is very simple. Test::Kwalitee does all of its work behind the scenes. The eval and exit lines exist to prevent the tests from attempting to run and failing for users who do not have the module installed.

Test::Kwalitee judges the kwalitee of a distribution on eight metrics:

See the documentation for changes to these metrics.

- Are the permissions of the files sane? Read-only files cause some installers difficulty.
- Are there any symbolic links in the distribution? They do not work on all filesystems.
- Is there a file to run to configure, build, and test the distribution?
- Is there a *MANIFEST* file listing all of the distribution files?
- Is there a *META.yml* file containing the distribution's metadata?
- Is there a *README* file?
- Are there any errors in the included POD?
- Does the distribution use any modules it has not declared as prerequisites?

If all of those tests pass, the module has decent kwalitee. Kwalitee doesn't guarantee that your code works well, or even at all, but it is a sign that you've bundled it properly.

What about...

Q: *Should I distribute this test with my other tests?*

A: Opinions vary. It's a useful test to run right before you release a new version of your distribution just to make sure that you haven't forgotten anything, but unless you're generating files that might change the code being tested on different platforms, this test won't reveal anything interesting when your users run it.

If you don't want to distribute the test and if you use Module::Build or ExtUtils::MakeMaker to bundle your distribution, add this test to your normal *t/* directory, but do not add it to your *MANIFEST* file. You can still run the test with make test, perl Build test, or prove, but make tardist, make dist, and perl Build dist will exclude it from the distribution file.

Q: *What if I disagree with a Kwalitee measurement and want to skip the test?*

A: See the documentation of Test::Kwalitee to learn how to disable certain tests.

## CHAPTER 5

Testing Untestable Code

One of the precepts of good unit testing is to test individual pieces of code in isolation. Besides helping to ensure that your code works, this testing improves your design by decoupling unrelated modules and enforcing communication among well-defined and, hopefully, well-tested interfaces. It also makes debugging failed tests easier by reducing the number of failure points.

Testing in isolation is difficult, though. Most applications have some degree of interdependence between components, being the sum of individual pieces that don't always make sense when isolated from the whole. An important pattern of behavior in testing is *mocking*: replacing untestable or hard-to-test code with code that looks like the real thing but makes it easier to test. Perl's easygoing nature allows you to poke around in other people's code in the middle of a program without too much trouble.

This chapter's labs demonstrate how to change code—even if it doesn't belong to you or if it merely touches what you really want to test—in the middle of your tests. Though fiddling with symbol tables and replacing variables and subroutines is very powerful, it is also dangerous. It's too useful a tool not to consider, though. Here's when, why, and how to do it safely.

Overriding Built-ins

No matter how nice it might be to believe otherwise, not all of the world is under your control. This is particularly true when dealing with Perl's built-in operators and functions, which can wreak havoc on your psyche when you're trying to test your code fully. Your program may need to run a `system()` call and deal with failure gracefully, but how do you test that?

Start by redefining the problem.

How do I do that?

Suppose you have written a module to play songs on your computer. It consists of a class, SongPlayer, that holds a song and the application to use to play that song. It also has a method, play( ), that launches the application to play the song. Save the following code as *lib/SongPlayer.pm*:

```perl
package SongPlayer;

use strict;
use warnings;

use Carp;

sub new
{
    my ($class, %args) = @_;
    bless \%args, $class;
}

sub song
{
    my $self       = shift;
    $self->{song} = shift if @_;
    $self->{song};
}

sub player
{
    my $self         = shift;
    $self->{player} = shift if @_;
    $self->{player};
}

sub play
{
    my $self   = shift;
    my $player = $self->player();
    my $song   = $self->song();

    system( $player, $song ) == 0 or
        croak( "Couldn't launch $player for $song: $!\n" );
}

1;
```

Testing the constructor (new( )) and the two accessors (song( ) and player( )) is easy. Testing play( ) is more difficult for two reasons. First, it calls system( ), which relies on behavior outside of the testing environment. How can you know which songs and media players people will have on their systems? You *could* bundle samples with the tests, but trying to support a full-blown media player on all of your target systems and architectures could be painful. Second, system( ) has side effects. If it launches a graphical program, there's no easy way to control it from Perl. To continue the tests, the user will have to exit it manually—so much for automation.

How can you write this test portably?

When you don't have the world you want, change it. Save this test file as *songplayer.t*:

```perl
#!perl

use strict;
use warnings;

use lib 'lib';

use Test::More tests => 11;
use Test::Exception;

my $module - 'SongPlayer';
use_ok( $module ) or exit;

can_ok( $module, 'new' );
my $song = $module->new( song => 'RomanceMe.mp3', player => 'xmms' );
isa_ok( $song, $module );

can_ok( $song, 'song' );
is( $song->song(), 'RomanceMe.mp3',
    'song() should return song set in constructor' );

can_ok( $song, 'player' );
is( $song->player(), 'xmms',
    'player() should return player set in constructor' );

can_ok( $song, 'play' );

{
    package SongPlayer;

    use subs 'system';

    package main;

    my $fail = 0;
    my @args;

    *SongPlayer::system = sub
    {
        @args = @_;
        return $fail;
    };
```

```
            lives_ok { $song->play() } 'play() should live if launching succeeds';

            is_deeply( \@args, [qw( xmms RomanceMe.mp3 )],
                'play() should launch player for song' );

            $fail = 1;
            throws_ok { $song->play() } qr/Couldn't launch xmms for RomanceMe.mp3/,
                '... throwing exception if launching fails';
        }
```

Run it with *prove*:

```
$ prove songplayer.t
songplayer....ok

All tests successful.
Files=1, Tests=11,  0 wallclock secs ( 0.10 cusr +  0.01 csys =  0.11 CPU)
```

What just happened?

Instead of launching xmms to play the song, the test overrode the system()
operator with a normal Perl subroutine. How did that happen?

The subs pragma allows you to make forward declarations of subroutines. It tells Perl to expect user-defined subroutines of the given names.
This changes how Perl reacts when it encounters those names. In effect,
this snippet:

```
use subs 'system';
```

hides the built-in system() in favor of a user-defined system(), even
though the definition happens much later as the test runs!

The test file performs one trick in using the subs pragma. It changes to
the SongPlayer package to execute the pragma there, and then changes
back to the main package. The other interesting part of the code is the
definition of the new system() function:

```
my $fail = 0;
my @args;

*SongPlayer::system = sub
{
    @args = @_;
    return $fail;
};
```

It's a closure, closing over the $fail and @args variables. Both the
enclosing block and the function can access the same lexical variables.
Setting $fail in the block changes what the function will return. The

*The forward
declaration could
take place at the
top of the test
file; it's in the
play() test for
clarity.*

mocked system() function sets @args based on the arguments it receives. Together, they allow the test to check what play() passes to system() and to verify that play() does the right thing based on the dummied-up return value of the mocked function.

Mocking system() allows the test to force a failure without the tester having to figure out a failure condition that will always run on every supported platform.

What about...

Q: *This seems invasive. Is there another way to do it without overriding system()?*

A: You can't easily undo overriding. If you cannot isolate the scope of the overriding well—whether in a block or a separate test file, this can be troublesome.

There's an alternative, in this case. Save the following test file as *really_play.t*:

```perl
#!perl

use strict;
use warnings;

use lib 'lib';

use Test::More tests => 5;
use Test::Exception;

my $module = 'SongPlayer';
use_ok( $module ) or exit;

my $song = $module->new( song => '77s_OneMoreTime.ogg',
    player => 'mpg321' );

$song->song( 'pass.pl' );
is( $song->song(), 'pass.pl',
    'song() should update song member, if set' );

$song->player( $^X );
is( $song->player(), $^X,
    'player() should update player member, if set' );

lives_ok { $song->play() } 'play() should launch program and live';

$song->song( 'fail.pl' );
```

The special variable $^X holds the path to the currently executing Perl binary. See perldoc perlvar.

```
dies_ok { $song->play( ) }
    'play( ) should croak if program launch fails';
```

Instead of setting the song and player to an actual song and player, this code uses the currently executing Perl binary and sets the song to either *pass.pl* or *fail.pl*. Save this code to *pass.pl*:

```
exit 0;
```

and this code as *fail.pl*:

```
exit 1;
```

Now when play( ) calls system( ), it runs the equivalent of the command perl pass.pl or perl fail.pl, checking the command's exit code.

This kind of testing is more implicit; if something goes wrong, it can be difficult to isolate the invalid assumption. Was the name of the file wrong? Was its exit value wrong? However, redefining part of Perl can be treacherous, even if you put the overriding code in its own test file to minimize the damage of violating encapsulation. Using fake programs is gentler and may have fewer unexpected side effects.

Both approaches are appropriate at different times. When you have precise control of how your code communicates with the outside world, it's often simpler to run fake programs through the system( ) command, for example. When it's tedious to exercise all of the necessary behavior of the external program or resource, mocking is easier.

Mocking Modules

Sometimes two or more pieces of code play very nicely together. This is great—until you want to test them in isolation. While it's good to write testable code, you shouldn't have to go through contortions to make it possible to write tests. Sometimes it's okay for your tests to poke through the abstractions, just a little bit, to make sure that your code works the way you think it ought to work.

Being a little bit tricky in your test code—in the proper places and with the proper precautions—can make both your code and your tests much simpler and easier to test.

How do I do that?

Suppose that you want to search for types of links in HTML documents. You've defined a class, LinkFinder, whose objects contain the HTML to search as well as an internal parser object that does the actual HTML parsing. For convenience, the class uses the LWP::Simple library to fetch HTML from a web server when provided a bare URI.

Save the following code as *lib/LinkFinder.pm*:

```perl
package LinkFinder;

use URI;
use LWP::Simple ();
use HTML::TokeParser::Simple;

sub new
{
    my ($class, $html) = @_;
    my $uri            = URI->new( $html );

    if ($uri->scheme())
    {
        $html = LWP::Simple::get( $uri->as_string() );
    }

    my $self = bless { html => $html }, $class;
    $self->reset();
}

sub parser
{
    my $self = shift;
    return $self->{parser};
}

sub html
{
    my $self = shift;
    return $self->{html};
}

sub find_links
{
    my ($self, $uri) = @_;
    my $parser       = $self->parser();

    my @links;

    while (my $token = $parser->get_token() )
    {
        next unless $token->is_start_tag( 'a' );
        next unless $token->get_attr( 'href' ) =~ /\Q$uri\E/;
        push @links, $self->find_text();
    }

    return @links;
}
```

```perl
sub find_text
{
    my $self   = shift;
    my $parser = $self->parser();

    while (my $token = $parser->get_token())
    {
        next unless $token->is_text();
        return $token->as_is();
    }

    return;
}

sub reset
{
    my $self         = shift;
    my $html         = $self->html();
    $self->{parser} = HTML::TokeParser::Simple->new( string => $html );

    return $self;
}

1;
```

Save the following test file as *findlinks.t*:

```perl
#!perl

use strict;
use warnings;

use lib 'lib';

use Test::More tests => 11;
use Test::MockModule;

my $module = 'LinkFinder';
use_ok( $module ) or exit;
my $html   = do { local $/; <DATA> };

my $vanity = $module->new( $html );
isa_ok( $vanity, $module );
is( $vanity->html(), $html, 'new() should allow HTML passed in from string'
);

{
    my $uri;
    my $lwp = Test::MockModule->new( 'LWP::Simple' );
    $lwp->mock( get => sub ($) { $uri = shift; $html } );

    $vanity = $module->new( 'http://www.example.com/somepage.html' );
    is( $vanity->html(), $html, '... or from URI if passed' );
```

The test declares $uri outside of the mocked subroutine to make the variable visible outside of the subroutine.

```
        is( $uri, 'http://www.example.com/somepage.html',
            '... URI passed into constructor' );
    }

    my @results = $vanity->find_links( 'http' );
    is( @results, 3, 'find_links() should find all matching links' );
    is( $results[0], 'one author',      '... in order'          );
    is( $results[1], 'another author', '... of appearance'      );
    is( $results[2], 'a project',       '... in document'       );

    $vanity->reset();
    @results    = $vanity->find_links( 'perl' );
    is( @results, 1,              'reset() should reset parser'  );
    is( $results[0], 'a project', '... allowing more link finding' );

    __DATA__
    <html>
    <head><title>some page</title>
    <body>
    <p><a href="http://wgz.org/chromatic/">one author</a></p>
    <p><a href="http://longworth.com/">another author</a></p>
    <p><a href="http://qa.perl.org/">a project</a></p>
    </body>
```

See Special
Literals in perldoc
perldata to learn
about __DATA__.

Run it with *prove*:

```
$ prove findlinks.t
findlinks....ok
All tests successful.
Files=1, Tests=11,  0 wallclock secs ( 0.21 cusr +  0.02 csys =  0.23 CPU)
```

What just happened?

When LinkFinder creates a new object, it creates a new URI object from the $html parameter. If $html contains actual HTML, the URI object won't have a scheme. If, however, $html contains a URL to an HTTP or FTP site *containing* HTML, it will have a scheme. In that case, it uses LWP::Simple to fetch the HTML.

You can't rely on having a reliable network connection every time you want to run the tests, nor should you worry that the remote site will be down or that someone has changed the HTML and your tests will fail. You *could* run a small web server to test against, but there's an easier solution.

The Test::MockModule module takes most of the tedium out of overriding subroutines in other packages (see "Overriding Live Code," later in this chapter). Because LinkFinder uses LWP::Simple::get() directly, without importing it, the easiest option is to mock get() in the LWP::Simple package.

*The anonymous
subroutine has a
prototype to
match that of
LWP::Simple::get().
Perl will warn
about a prototype
mismatch without
it. You only need a
prototype if the
subroutine being
mocked has one.*

The test creates a new Test::MockModule object representing LWP::
Simple. That doesn't actually change anything; only the call to mock( )
does. The two arguments passed to mock( ) are the name of the subroutine to override—get, in this case—and an anonymous subroutine to use
for the overriding.

Within the new scope, all of LinkFinder's calls to LWP::Simple::get( )
actually call the anonymous subroutine instead, storing the argument in
$uri and returning the example HTML from the end of the test file.

The rest of the test is straightforward.

*What if you
decide to import
get( ) in
LinkFinder after
all? Pass
'LinkFinder' to the
Test::MockModule
constructor
instead.*

What about...

Q: *What if you write mostly object-oriented code? How do you mock
classes and objects?*

A: See "Mocking Objects," next.

Mocking Objects

Some programs rely heavily on the use of objects, eschewing global variables and functions for loosely-coupled, well-encapsulated, and strongly
polymorphic designs. This kind of code can be easier to maintain and
understand—and to test. Well-factored code that adheres to intelligent
interfaces between objects makes it possible to reuse and substitute
equivalent implementations—including testing components.

This lab demonstrates how to create and use mock objects to test the
inputs and outputs of code.

How do I do that?

The following code defines an object that sends templated mail to its
recipients. Save it as *lib/MailTemplate.pm*:

```
package MailTemplate;

use strict;
use Email::Send 'SMTP';

sub new
{
    my ($class, %args) = @_;
    bless \%args, $class;
}
```

```perl
BEGIN
{
    no strict 'refs';

    for my $accessor (qw( message recipients sender sender_address server ))
    {
        *{ $accessor } = sub
        {
            my $self   = shift;
            return $self->{$accessor};
        };
    }
}

sub add_recipient
{
    my ($self, $name, $address) = @_;
    my $recipients              = $self->recipients();
    $recipients->{$name}        = $address;
}

sub deliver
{
    my $self       = shift;
    my $recipients = $self->recipients();

    while (my ($name, $address) = each %$recipients)
    {
        my $message = $self->format_message( $name, $address );
        send( 'SMTP', $message, $self->server() );
    }
}

sub format_message
{
    my ($self, $name, $address) = @_;

    my $message     = $self->message();
    my %data        =
    (
        name           => $name,
        address        => $address,
        sender         => $self->sender(),
        sender_address => $self->sender_address(),
    );

    $message =~ s/{(\w+)}/$data{$1}/g;
    return $message;
}

1;
```

The BEGIN trick here is like using AUTOLOAD to generate accessors, except that it runs at compile time for only those accessors specified.

Using this module is easy. To send out personalized mail to several recipients, create a new object, passing the name of your SMTP server, your name, your address, a templated message, and a hash of recipient names and addresses.

Testing this module, on the other hand, could be tricky; it uses Email:: Send (specifically Email::Send::SMTP) to send messages. You don't want to rely on having a network connection in place, nor do you want to send mail to some poor soul every time someone runs the tests, especially while you develop them.

What's the answer?

Save the following test code to *mailtemplate.t*:

```perl
#!perl

use strict;
use warnings;

use Test::More tests => 23;
use Test::MockObject;

use lib 'lib';

$INC{'Net/SMTP.pm'} = 1;
my $module      = 'MailTemplate';
my $message     = do { local $/; <DATA> };

use_ok( $module ) or exit;

can_ok( $module, 'new' );
my $mt = $module->new(
    server          => 'smtp.example.com',
    sender          => 'A. U. Thor',
    message         => $message,
    sender_address => 'author@example.com',
    recipients      => { Bob => 'bob@example.com' },
);
isa_ok( $mt, $module );

can_ok( $mt, 'server' );
is( $mt->server(), 'smtp.example.com',
    'server() should return server set in constructor' );

can_ok( $mt, 'add_recipient' );
$mt->add_recipient( Alice => 'alice@example.com' );

can_ok( $mt, 'recipients' );
is_deeply( $mt->recipients(),
        { Alice => 'alice@example.com', Bob => 'bob@example.com' },
        'recipients() should return all recipients' );
```

```perl
    can_ok( $mt, 'deliver' );

    my $smtp = Test::MockObject->new();
    $smtp->fake_module( 'Net::SMTP', new => sub { $smtp } );
    $smtp->set_true( qw( mail to data -quit ) );
    $mt->deliver();

    my %recipients =
    (
        Alice => 'alice@example.com',
        Bob   => 'bob@example.com',
    );

    while (my ($name, $address) = each %recipients)
    {
        my ($method, $args) = $smtp->next_call();
        is( $method,     'mail',                 'deliver() should open a mail' );
        is( $args->[1], 'author@example.com','... setting the From address' );

        ($method, $args) = $smtp->next_call();
        is( $method,     'to',                   '... then the To address' ),
        is( $args->[1], $address,                '... for the recipient'   );

        ($method, $args) = $smtp->next_call(),
        is( $method,       'data',         '... sending the message'   );
        like( $args->[1], qr/Hello, $name/,   '... greeting the recipient' );
        like( $args->[1], qr/Love,.A. U. Thor/s,
                '... and signing sender name' );
    }

    __DATA__
To: {address}
From: {sender_address}
Subject: A Test Message

Hello, {name}!

You won't actually receive this message!

Love,
{sender}
```

Don't make assumptions about hash ordering; you'll have random test failures when you least expect them. Sort all data retrieved from hashes if the order matters to you.

Then run it:

```
$ prove mailtemplate.t
mailtemplate....ok
All tests successful.
Files=1, Tests=23,  1 wallclock secs ( 0.16 cusr +  0.02 csys =  0.18 CPU)
```

What just happened?

The test file starts with a curious line:

```perl
$INC{'Net/SMTP.pm'} = 1;
```

This line prevents the module from (eventually) loading the Net::SMTP module, which Email::Send::SMTP uses internally. %INC is a global variable that contains entries for all loaded modules. When Perl loads a module, such as Test::More, it converts the module name into a Unix file path and adds it to %INC as a new key. The next time Perl tries to load a file with that name, it checks the hash. If there's an entry, it refuses to load the file again.

If Perl doesn't actually load Net::SMTP, where does the code for that package come from? Test::MockObject provides it:

```perl
my $smtp = Test::MockObject->new();
$smtp->fake_module( 'Net::SMTP', new => sub { $smtp } );
```

The first line creates a new mock object. The second tells Test:: MockObject to insert a new function, new(), into the Net::SMTP namespace. Because Email::Send::SMTP uses Net::SMTP::new() to retrieve an object and assumes that it has received a Net::SMTP object, this is the perfect place to substitute a mock object for the real thing.

Of course, when Email::Send::SMTP tries to call methods on the mock object, it won't do the right thing unless the mock object mocks those methods. Test::MockObject has several helper methods that mock methods on the object. set_true() defines a list of methods with the given names:

```perl
$smtp->set_true( qw( mail to data -quit ) );
```

Each method mocked this way returns a true value. More importantly, they all log their calls by default, unless you prefix their names with the minus character (-). Now Email::Send::SMTP can call mail(), to(), data(), and quit(), and $smtp will log information about the calls for all but the last.

Logging is important if you want to see if the module being tested sends out the data you expect. In this case, it's important to test that the message goes to the correct recipients from the correct sender, with the template filled out appropriately. Use next_call() to retrieve information about the logged calls:

```perl
my ($method, $args) = $smtp->next_call();
is( $method,    'mail',                 'deliver() should open a mailer' );
is( $args->[1], 'author@example.com', '... setting the From address'   );
```

In list context, next_call() retrieves the name of the next method called, as well as an array reference containing the arguments to the call. These two tests check that the next method called is the expected one and that the first argument, after the invocant, of course, is the expected From address.

What about...

Q: *This test code seems to depend on the order of the calls within* `Email::Send::SMTP`. *Isn't this fragile? What if changes to the module break the tests?*

A: That's one drawback of mock objects; they rely on specific knowledge of the internals of the code being tested. Instead of testing merely that a piece of code does the right thing, sometimes they go further to test *how* it does what it does.

When possible, designing your code to be more testable will make it more flexible. `MailTemplate` would be easier to test if its constructor took an object that could send mail. The test could then pass a mock object in through the `new()` call and perform its checks on that.

However, the real world isn't always that convenient. Sometimes testing a few parts of a large application with mock objects is the best way to test every part in isolation.

Q: *I looked at the* `Test::MockObject` *documentation and still don't understand how to use it. What am I missing?*

A: See "A Test::MockObject Illustrated Example" (*http://www.perl.com/pub/a/2002/07/10/tmo.html*) and "Perl Code Kata: Mocking Objects" (*http://www.perl.com/pub/a/2005/04/07/mockobject_kata.html*) for more examples.

Q: *Do I have to mock all of an object? I only need to change a small part of it.*

A: Good thinking. See "Partially Mocking Objects," next.

Partially Mocking Objects

Mock objects are useful because they give so much control over the testing environment. That great power also makes them potentially dangerous. You may write fantastic tests that appear to cover an entire codebase only to have the code fail in real situations when the unmocked world behaves differently.

Sometimes it's better to mock only part of an object, using as much real code as possible. When you have well-designed and well-factored classes and methods, use `Test::MockObject::Extends` to give you control over tiny pieces of code you want to change, leaving the rest of it alone.

How do I do that?

Consider the design of a computer-controlled jukebox for your music collection. Suppose that it holds records, CDs, and MP3 files, with a counter for each item to track popularity. The well-designed jukebox separates storing individual pieces of music from playing them. It has three modules: Jukebox, which provides the interface to select and play music; Library, which stores and retrieves music; and Music, which represents a piece of music.

The Jukebox class is simple:

```perl
package Jukebox;

use strict;
use warnings;

sub new
{
    my ($class, $library) = @_;
    bless { library => $library }, $class;
}

sub library
{
    my $self = shift;
    return $self->{library};
}

sub play_music
{
    my ($self, $medium, $title) = @_;

    my $class                  = ucfirst( lc( $medium ) );
    my $library                = $self->library();
    my $music                  = $library->load( $class, $title );
    return unless $music;

    $music->play();
    $music->add_play();

    $library->save( $music, $title, $music );
}

1;
```

Library is a little more complicated:

```perl
package Library;

use strict;
use warnings;

use Carp 'croak';
use File::Spec::Functions qw( catdir catfile );
```

```perl
sub new
{
    my ($class, $path) = @_;
    bless \$path, $class;
}

sub path
{
    my $self = shift;
    return $$self;
}

sub load
{
    my ($self, $type, $id) = @_;
    my $directory          = $self->find_dir( $type );
    my $data               = $self->read_file( $directory, $id );
    bless $data, $type;
}

sub save
{
    my ($self, $object, $id) = @_;
    my $directory            = $self->find_dir( $object->type() );
    $self->save_file( $directory, $id, $object->data() );
}

sub find_dir
{
    my ($self, $type) = @_;
    my $path          = $self->path();
    my $directory     = catdir( $path, $type );
    croak( "Unknown directory '$directory'" ) unless -d $directory;
    return $directory;
}

sub read_file {}
sub save_file {}

1;
```

Finally, the Music class is simple:

```perl
package Music;

use strict;
use warnings;

BEGIN
{
    @Cd::ISA     = 'Music';
    @Mp3::ISA    = 'Music';
    @Record::ISA = 'Music';
}
```

```perl
sub new
{
    my ($class, $title) = @_;
    bless { title => $title, count => 0 }, $class;
}

sub add_play
{
    my $self = shift;
    $self->{count}++;
}

sub data
{
    my $self = shift;
    return \%$self;
}

sub play {}
sub type { ref( $_[0] ) }

1;
```

Given all of this code, one way to test Jukebox is to mock only a few methods of Library: find_dir( ), read_file( ), and save_file( ).

Save the following file as *jukebox.t*:

```perl
#!perl

use strict;
use warnings;

use Library;
use Music;

use Test::More tests => 13;
use Test::Exception;
use Test::MockObject::Extends;

my $lib      = Library->new( 'my_files' );
my $mock_lib = Test::MockObject::Extends->new( $lib );

my $module    = 'Jukebox';
use_ok( $module ) or exit;

can_ok( $module, 'new' );
my $jb = $module->new( $mock_lib );
isa_ok( $jb, $module );

can_ok( $jb, 'library' );
is( $jb->library(), $mock_lib,
    'library() should return library set in constructor' );
```

```
can_ok( $jb, 'play_music' );

$mock_lib->set_always( -path => 'my_path' );
throws_ok { $jb->play_music( 'mp3', 'Romance Me' ) } qr/Unknown directory/,
    'play_music() should throw exception if it cannot find directory';

$mock_lib->set_always( -find_dir => 'my_directory' );
$mock_lib->set_always( read_file => { file => 'my_file' } );
$mock_lib->set_true( 'save_file' );

lives_ok { $jb->play_music( 'CD', 'Films For Radio' ) }
    '... but no exception if it can find it';

$mock_lib->called_ok( 'read_file' );
my ($method, $args) = $mock_lib->next_call( 2 );
is( $method,      'save_file',       'play_music() should also save file' );
is( $args->[1], 'my_directory',    '... saving to the proper directory' );
is( $args->[2], 'Films For Radio', '... with the proper id'         );
is( $args->[3]{count}, 1,          '... and the proper count'       );
```

Run the test with *prove*. All tests should pass.

What just happened?

The code for mocking objects should look familiar (see "Mocking Objects," earlier in this chapter), but the code to create the mock object is different. In particular, this test loads the Library module and instantiates an actual object before passing it to the Test::MockObject::Extends constructor.

Any methods called on the mock object that it doesn't currently mock will pass through to the object being mocked. That is, without adding any other methods to it, calling save() or find_dir() on $mock_lib will actually call the real methods from Library. That's why the first call to play_music() throws an exception: the directory name created in Library::find_dir() doesn't exist.

The test then mocks find_dir() so that subsequent tests will pass. Next it mocks the read_file() and save_file() methods.

Because Library has put all of the actual file-handling code in three methods, it's easy to test that Jukebox does the right thing without worrying about reading or writing files that may not exist or that the test may not have permission to access.

Note which mocked methods the test logs and which methods it doesn't. This is a useful technique when you want to test calls to some methods but not others.

When testing Music and its subclasses, it might be useful to mock play() too, depending on its implementation.

What about...

Q: *How can you ensure that loading and saving work correctly?*

A: That's important, too, but that belongs in the tests for Library. This test exercises Jukebox; it interacts with Library only as far as Jukebox must use the Library interface appropriately.

Using mock objects is still somewhat fragile. In this example, if someone changes the interface of the methods in Library, the mock object may need to change. However, mocking only a few, small pieces of a well-designed object reduces the coupling between the mock object and the original object. This makes tests more robust.

Overriding Live Code

Plenty of useful modules do their work procedurally, without the modularity of functions and objects. Many modules, written before object orientation became popular, use package variables to control their behavior. To test your code fully, sometimes you have to reach inside those packages to change their variables. Tread lightly, though. Tricky testing code is harder to write and harder to debug.

How do I do that?

Suppose that you have a simple logging package. Its single subroutine, log_message( ), takes a message and logs it to a filehandle. It also adds a time and date stamp to the start of the message and information about the function's caller to the end, if two package global variables, $REPORT_TIME and $REPORT_CALLER, are true.

Save the following code to *lib/Logger.pm*:

```perl
package Logger;

use strict;

our $OUTPUT_FH     = *STDERR;
our $REPORT_TIME   = 1;
our $REPORT_CALLER = 1;

sub log_message
{
    my ($package, $file, $line) = caller();
    my $time                    = localtime();

    my $message                 = '';
    $message                    .= "[$time] " if $REPORT_TIME;
    $message                    .= shift;
```

```perl
    $message                         .= " from $package:$line in $file"
                                        if $REPORT_CALLER;
    $message                         .= "\n";

    write_message( $message );
}

sub write_message
{
    my $message = shift;
    print $OUTPUT_FH $message;
}

1;
```

Fortunately, the module is simple enough, so it's straightforward to test. The difficult part is figuring out how to capture the output from write_message( ). You *could* test both functions at the same time, but it's easier to test features in isolation, both to improve your test robustness and to reduce complications.

Save the following code to *log_message.t*:

```perl
#!perl

use strict;
use warnings;

use lib 'lib';

use Test::More tests => 6;
use Test::MockModule;

my $module = 'Logger';
use_ok( $module ) or exit;

can_ok( $module, 'log_message' );

{
    local $Logger::REPORT_TIME   = 0;
    local $Logger::REPORT_CALLER = 0;

    my $message;
    my $logger = Test::MockModule->new( 'Logger' );
    $logger->mock( write_message => sub { $message = shift } );

    Logger::log_message( 'no decoration' );
    is( $message, "no decoration\n",
        'log_message() should not add time or caller unless requested' );

    $Logger::REPORT_TIME   = 1;
    Logger::log_message( 'time only' );
    (my $time = localtime()) =~ s/:\d+ /:\\d+ /;
    like( $message, qr/^\[$time\] time only$/,
        '... adding time if requested' );
```

```
$Logger::REPORT_CALLER = 1;
my $line                = __LINE__ + 1;
Logger::log_message( 'time and caller' );
like( $message, qr/^\[$time\] time and caller from main:$line in $0$/,
    '... adding time and caller, if both requested' );

$Logger::REPORT_TIME   = 0;
$line                  = __LINE__ + 1;
Logger::log_message( 'caller only' );
like( $message, qr/^caller only from main:$line in $0$/,
    '... adding caller only if requested' );
}
```

Run it with *prove*:

```
$ prove log_message.t
log_message....ok
All tests successful.
Files=1, Tests=6,  0 wallclock secs ( 0.10 cusr +  0.00 csys =  0.10 CPU)
```

What just happened?

See "Temporary
Values via local( )"
in perldoc perlsub
for more details
on localizing global
symbols. This is a
big topic related
to Perl's inner
workings.

The first interesting section of code, in the block following can_ok( ),
localizes the two package variables from Logger, $REPORT_TIME and
$REPORT_CALLER.

The benefit of local( ) is that it allows temporary values for global symbols, even those from other packages. Outside of that scope, the variables retain their previous values. Though it's easy to assign to them
without localizing them, it's nicer to encapsulate those changes in a new
scope and let Perl restore their old values. Inside the scope of the
localized variables, the test uses Test::MockModule's mock( ) method to
install a temporary write_message( ) only for the duration of the lexical
scope.

With the new write_message( ) temporarily in place, the message that
log_message( ) creates will end up in the $message variable, which
makes it easy to test the four possible combinations of reporting values.
The rest of the code is straightforward, with two exceptions.

Note how the regular expression changes the output of localtime( ) to
make the test less sensitive about timing issues; the test shouldn't fail if
it happens to run just at the boundary of a second. As it is, there is still a
small race condition if the minute happens to turn over, but the potential
for failure is much smaller now.

The other new piece is the use of the __LINE__ directive and the special
variable $0 to verify that log_message( ) reports the proper calling line
number and filename.

What about...

Q: *What's the best way to test* write_message()?

A: write_message() performs two different potential actions. First, it writes to the STDERR filehandle by default. Second, it writes to the filehandle in $OUTPUT_FH if someone has set it. The Test::Output module from the CPAN is useful for both tests.

Save the following code to *write_message.t*:

```perl
#!perl

use strict;
use warnings;

use lib 'lib';

use Test::More tests => 3;
use Test::Output;
use Test::Output::Tie;

my $module = 'Logger';
use_ok( $module ) or exit;

stderr_is( sub { Logger::write_message( 'To STDERR!' ) }, 'To STDERR!',
    'write_message() should write to STDERR by default' );

{
    local *Logger::OUTPUT_FH;

    my $out              = tie *Logger::OUTPUT_FH, 'Test::Output::Tie';
    $Logger::OUTPUT_FH = *Logger::OUTPUT_FH;

    Logger::write_message( 'To $out!' );
    is( $out->read(), 'To $out!', '... or to $OUTPUT_FH, if set' );
}
```

Run it with *prove*:

```
$ prove write_message.t
write_message....ok
All tests successful.
Files=1, Tests=3,  0 wallclock secs ( 0.11 cusr +  0.00 csys =  0.11
    CPU)
```

Test::Output's stderr_is() is handy for testing Logger's default behavior. Its only quirk is that its first argument must be an anonymous subroutine. Otherwise, it's as simple as can be.

Testing that write_message() prints to other filehandles is only slightly more complex. As with the tests for write_message(), the goal is to capture the output in a variable. Test::Output uses a

Tying a variable with tie() is like subclassing a module; it presents the same interface but performs different behavior. See perldoc perltie to learn more.

module called Test::Output::Tie internally to do exactly that. It ties a filehandle that captures all data printed to it and returns this data when you call its read( ) method.

Overriding Operators Everywhere

Overriding Perl operators locally is an important skill to know. Sometimes it's not sufficient, though. Consider the case of code that calls exit( ) occasionally. That's anathema to testing, but you don't have to give up on unit testing altogether. If you can isolate the affected code to a few places in the program, you can test that code in isolation, redefining the systemwide exit( ) function to do what you want.

How do I do that?

Take the example of a module that enforces password protection for users. Save the following code as *PasswordKeeper.pm* in your library directory:

```perl
package PasswordKeeper;

sub new
{
    my ($class, $username) = @_;
    my $password          = $class->encrypt( $username );
    bless
    {
        user     => $username,
        tries    => 0,
        password => $password,
    }, $class;
}

sub verify
{
    my ($self, $guess) = @_;

    return 1 if $self->encrypt( $guess ) eq $self->{password};

    $self->{tries}++;
    exit if $self->{tries} == 3;

    return 0;
}

sub encrypt
{
    my ($class, $password) = @_;
```

```
         return scalar reverse $password;
     }

     1;
```

That exit() looks a little dangerous, but at least it occurs in only one method. Save the following test file as *pkeeper_exit.t*:

```
#!perl

use strict;
use warnings;

use lib 'lib';

use Test::More tests -> 3;

my $exited;
BEGIN { *CORE::GLOBAL::exit = sub { $exited++ } };

my $module = 'PasswordKeeper';
use_ok( $module ) or die( "Could not load $module" );

my $mel = $module->new( 'Melanie' );
isa_ok( $mel, $module );

$mel->verify( $_ ) for qw( buffy babycat milkyway );
is( $exited, 1, 'verify() should exit if it receives three bad passwords' );
```

Run it with *prove*:

```
$ prove pkeeper_exit.t
pkeeper_exit...ok
All tests successful.
Files=1, Tests=3,  0 wallclock secs ( 0.07 cusr +  0.02 csys =  0.09 CPU)
```

What just happened?

PasswordKeeper works by taking a username and encrypting it to make a password when it creates a new object. The verify() method takes a potential password, encrypts it, and compares it against the stored password. If they match, the method returns true. Otherwise, it increases a counter of failed attempts and exits the program if someone has tried three unsuccessful passwords.

That exiting is important behavior to test. The test file starts by defining exit() in the special CORE::GLOBAL namespace. That overrides exit() *everywhere*, not just in main, where the code of the test file lives, or in PasswordKeeper. The new exit() increments the $exited variable, so the third test in the file can check that PasswordKeeper called exit() once for three failed password attempts.

Don't use this encryption technique for data you care about. See the Crypt namespace on the CPAN for better options.

Assume that another test file exercises PasswordKeeper's non-exiting behavior.

Read perldoc perlsub and perldoc perlvar to learn more about CORE::GLOBAL. This is very powerful, so use it with care.

What about...

Q: *What's the advantage of overriding something everywhere instead of in a small scope?*

A: You might not be able to localize all of the calls to exit( ) (or system( ), die( ), etc.) into one place in one module of the code you're testing. In those situations, overriding the troublesome operator in a single test file that exercises the behavior can turn previously difficult code into testable code.

Make this test file small, so that it exercises only the code paths that cause the exiting. This will minimize the chances of unexpected behavior from your global overriding. If you can't modify the code you're testing to make it easier to test, at least you can encapsulate the tricky code into individual test files.

## CHAPTER 6

Testing Databases

Many programs need to work with external data. Given Perl's powerful and useful modules for database access, many programs use relational databases, simple flat files, and everything in between. It's in those places, where the real world and your program interact, that you need the most tests.

Fortunately, the same testing tools and techniques used elsewhere make testing databases and database access possible. The labs in this chapter explore some of the scenarios that you may encounter with applications that rely on external data storage and provide ideas and solutions to make them testable and reliable.

Shipping Test Databases

Many modern applications store data in databases for reasons of security, abstraction, and maintainability. This is often good programming, but it presents another challenge for testing; anything outside of the application itself is harder to test. How do you know how to connect to the database? How do you know which database the user will use?

Fortunately, Perl's DBI module, a few testing tools, and a little cleverness make it possible to be confident that your code does what it should do both inside the database and out.

Often, it's enough to run the tests against a very simple database full of testable data. DBI works with several database driver modules that are small and easy to use, including DBD::CSV and DBD::AnyData. The driver and DBI work together to provide the same interface that you'd have with a fully relational database system. If you've abstracted away creating and connecting to the database in a single place that you can control or mock, you can create a database handle in your test and make the code use that instead of the actual connection.

How do I do that?

For a better version of the Users module, see Class::DBI from the CPAN.

Imagine that you store user information in a database. The Users module creates and fetches user information from a single table; it is a factory for User objects. Save the following code in your library directory as *Users.pm*:

```perl
package Users;

use strict;
use warnings;

my $dbh;

sub set_db
{
    my ($self, $connection) = @_;
    $dbh                    = $connection;
}

sub fetch
{
    my ($self, $column, $value) = @_;

    my $sth = $dbh->prepare(
        "SELECT id, name, age FROM users WHERE $column = ?" );

    $sth->execute( $value );

    return unless my ($id, $name, $age) = $sth->fetchrow_array();
    bless { id => $id, name => $name, age => $age, _db => $self }, 'User';
}

sub create
{
    my ($self, %attributes) = @_;
    my $sth                 = $dbh->prepare(
        'INSERT INTO users (name, age) VALUES (?, ?)'
    );

    $sth->execute( @attributes{qw( name age )} );
    $attributes{id} = $dbh->last_insert_id( undef, undef, 'users', 'id' );
    bless \%attributes, 'User';
}

package User;

our $AUTOLOAD;
```

```
sub AUTOLOAD
{
    my $self      = shift;
    my ($member) = $AUTOLOAD =~ /::(\w+)\z/;
    return $self->{$member} if exists $self->{$member};
}

1;
```

A better—if longer—version of this code would add a constructor to the Users object and set a per-object database handle.

Note the use of the set_db( ) function at the start of User. It stores a single database handle for the entire class.

The Users package is simple; it contains accessors for the name, age, and id fields associated with the user. The code itself is just a thin layer around a few database calls. Testing it should be easy. Save the following test file as *users.t*:

```
#!perl

use strict;
use warnings;

use DBI;

my $dbh = DBI->connect( 'dbi:SQLite:dbname=test_data' );
{
    local $/ = ";\n";
    $dbh->do( $_ ) while <DATA>;
}

use Test::More tests -> 10;

my $module = 'Users';
use_ok( $module ) or exit;

can_ok( $module, 'set_db' );
$module->set_db( $dbh );

can_ok( $module, 'fetch' );
my $user = $module->fetch( id => 1 );
isa_ok( $user, 'User' );
is( $user->name(), 'Randy', 'fetch() should fetch proper user by id' );

$user    = $module->fetch( name => 'Ben' );
is( $user->id(), 2, '... or by name' );

can_ok( $module, 'create' );
$user    = $module->create( name => 'Emily', age => 23 );
isa_ok( $user, 'User' );
is( $user->name(), 'Emily', 'create() should create and return new User' );
is( $user->id(), 3, '... with the correct id' );

__END__
```

```
BEGIN TRANSACTION;
DROP TABLE users;
CREATE TABLE users (
    id    int,
    name  varchar(25),
    age   int
);
INSERT INTO "users" VALUES(1, 'Randy', 27);
INSERT INTO "users" VALUES(2, 'Ben', 29);
COMMIT;
```

Run it with *prove* to see:

```
$ prove users.t
users....ok
All tests successful.
Files=1, Tests=10,  0 wallclock secs ( 0.17 cusr +  0.00 csys =  0.17 CPU)
```

What just happened?

The test starts off by loading the DBI module and connecting to a SQLite database with the DBD::SQLite driver. Then it reads in SQL stored at the end of the test file and executes each SQL command, separated by semicolons, individually. These commands create a users table and insert some sample data.

By the time the test calls Users->set_db( ), $dbh holds a connection to the SQLite database stored in *test_data*. All subsequent calls to Users will use this handle. From there, the rest of the tests call methods and check their return values.

SQLite is a simple but powerful relational database that stores all of its data in a single file.

What about...

Q: *This works great for testing code that uses a database, but what about code that changes information in the database?*

A: Suppose that you want to prove that Users::create( ) actually inserts information into the database. See "Testing Database Data," next.

Q: *Only simple SQL queries are compatible across databases. What if my code uses unportable or database-specific features?*

A: This technique works for the subset of SQL and database use that's portable across major databases. If your application uses things such as additions to SQL, special schema types, or stored procedures, using DBD::SQLite or DBD::AnyData may be inappropriate. In that case, testing against an equivalent database with test data or mocking the database is better. (See "Using Temporary Databases" and "Mocking Databases," later in this chapter.)

Testing Database Data

If your application is the only code that ever touches its database, then testing your abstractions is easy: test what you can store against what you can fetch. However, if your application uses the database to communicate with other applications, what's *in* the database is more important than what your code retrieves from it. In those cases, good testing requires you to examine the contents of the database directly.

Suppose that the Users module from "Shipping Test Databases" is part of a larger, multilanguage system for managing users in a company. If it were the only code that dealt with the underlying database, the existing tests there would suffice—the internal representation of the data can change as long as the external interface stays the same. As it is, other applications will rely on specific details of the appropriate tables and, for Users to work properly, it must conform to the expected structure.

Fortunately, Test::DatabaseRow provides tests for common database-related tasks.

How do I do that?

Save the following file as *users_db.t*:

```perl
#!perl

use lib 'lib';

use strict;
use warnings;

use DBI;

my $dbh = DBI->connect( 'dbi:SQLite:dbname=test_data' );
{
    local $/ = ";\n";
    $dbh->do( $_ ) while <DATA>;
}

use Test::More tests => 4;
use Test::DatabaseRow;

my $module = 'Users';
use_ok( $module ) or exit;
$module->set_db( $dbh );
$module->create( name => 'Emily', age => 23 );

local $Test::DatabaseRow::dbh = $dbh;
```

```
row_ok(
    sql   => 'SELECT count(*) AS count FROM users',
    tests => [ count => 3 ],
    label => 'create() should insert a row',
);

row_ok(
    table   => 'users',
    where   => [ name => 'Emily', age => 23 ],
    results => 1,
    label   => '... with the appropriate data',
);

row_ok(
    table => 'users',
    where => [ id => 3 ],
    tests => [ name => 'Emily', age => 23 ],
    label => '... and a new id',
);

__END__
BEGIN TRANSACTION;
DROP TABLE users;
CREATE TABLE users (
id   int,
name varchar(25),
age  int
);
INSERT INTO "users" VALUES(1, 'Randy', 27);
INSERT INTO "users" VALUES(2, 'Ben', 29);
COMMIT;
```

Run it with *prove*:

This is an actual failure from writing the test code. It happens.

```
$ prove users_db.t
users_db....ok 1/0#       Failed test (users_db.t at line 39)
# No matching row returned
# The SQL executed was:
#    SELECT * FROM users WHERE id = '3'
# on database 'dbname=test_data'
# Looks like you failed 1 tests of 4.
users_db....dubious
        Test returned status 1 (wstat 256, 0x100)
DIED. FAILED test 4
        Failed 1/4 tests, 75.00% okay
Failed Test Stat Wstat Total Fail  Failed  List of Failed
-------------------------------------------------------------------------------
users_db.t   1   256     4     1  25.00%  4
Failed 1/1 test scripts, 0.00% okay. 1/4 subtests failed, 75.00% okay.
```

Oops.

What just happened?

For some reason, the test failed. Fortunately, Test::DatabaseRow gives diagnostics on the SQL that failed. Before delving into the failure, it's important to understand how to use the module.

Test::DatabaseRow builds on Test::Builder and exports two functions, row_ok() and not_row_ok(). Both functions take several pieces of data, use them to build and execute a SQL statement, and test its results. To run the tests, the module needs a database handle. The localization and assignment to $Test::DatabaseRow::dbh accomplishes this.

The testing functions accept two different kinds of calls. The first call to row_ok() passes raw SQL as the sql parameter to execute. This test creates a user for Emily and checks that there are now three rows in the users table with the SQL count(*) function. The second argument, tests, is an array reference of checks to perform against the returned row. In effect, this asks the question, "Is the count column in this row equal to 3?" Finally, the label parameter is the test's description used in its output.

Passing raw SQL to row_ok() isn't always much of an advantage over performing the query directly. The technique in the second and third calls to row_ok is better—Test::DatabaseRow generates a query from the table and where arguments and sends the query. The table argument identifies the table to query. The where argument contains an array reference of columns and values to use to narrow down the query.

The where argument is more powerful than these examples suggest. See the documentation for more details.

There is another difference between the second and the third tests: the second passes a results argument. Test::DatabaseRow uses this as the number of results that the query should produce for the test to fail. There should be only one Emily of age 23 in the database.

Why, then, did the third test fail? Looking at the debug output, the generated SQL looks correct. Keeping the sample SQLite database around at the end of the test allows you to use the *sqlite* program to browse the data. If you have SQLite installed, run it with:

Installing DBD::SQLite doesn't install the sqlite program. You have to do that separately.

```
$ sqlite3 test_data
SQLite version 3.0.8
Enter ".help" for instructions
sqlite> select * from users;
1|Randy|27
2|Ben|29
 |Emily|23
```

Ahh, this reveals that the row for Emily has an empty id column. Looking at the table definition again (and searching the SQLite documentation), the bug is clear. SQLite only generates a unique identifier for INTEGER columns marked as primary key. Depending on the characteristics of the actual database, this may be a significant difference in the test database that might mask an actual bug in the application!

Revise the table definition in *users_db.t* to:

```
CREATE TABLE users (
id    INTEGER primary key,
name varchar(25),
age  int
);
```

Then run the tests again:

```
$ prove users_db.t
users_db....ok
All tests successful.
Files=1, Tests=4,  0 wallclock secs ( 0.17 cusr +  0.00 csys =  0.17 CPU)
```

What about...

Q: *What if there are other differences between the live database and the test database?*

A: Sometimes the differences between a simple database such as SQLite and a larger database such as PostgreSQL or MySQL are more profound than changing the column types. In these cases, the technique shown here won't work. Fear not, though. The next section, "Using Temporary Databases," shows another approach.

Q: *Is keeping the test database around between invocations a good idea?*

A: The DROP TABLE command is useful, but if there's no database there, it can cause spurious warnings. Also, it's bad practice to leave test-created files lying around for someone else to clean up. Although they're sometimes helpful for debugging, most of the time they're just clutter.

Another option is to delete the test database at the end of the test:

```
END
{
    1 while unlink 'test_data' unless $ENV{TEST_DEBUG};
}
```

This will delete the database file completely, even on versioned file-systems, unless you explicitly ask for debugging. Running the test normally will leave no trace. To keep the database around, use a command such as:

```
$ TEST_DEBUG=1 prove users_db.t
```

Using Temporary Databases

Some programs rely on very specific database features. For example, a PostgreSQL or MySQL administration utility needs a deep knowledge of the underlying database. Other programs, including web content management systems, create their own tables and insert configuration data into the databases. Testing such systems with DBD::CSV is inappropriate; you won't cover enough of the system to be worthwhile.

In such cases, the best way to test your code is to test against a live database—or, at least, a database containing actual data. If you're already creating database tables and rows with your installer, go a step further and create a test database with the same information.

How do I do that?

Assume that you have an application named My::App (saved as *lib/My/App.pm*) and a file *sql/schema.sql* that holds your database schema and some basic data. You want to create both the live and test database tables during the installation process, and you need to know how to connect to the database to do so. One way to do this is to create a custom Module::Build subclass that asks the user for configuration information and installs the database along with the application.

Save the following file to *build_lib/MyBuild.pm*:

```perl
package MyBuild;

use base 'Module::Build';

use DBI;
use File::Path;
use Data::Dumper;
use File::Spec::Functions;

sub create_config_file
{
    my $self    = shift;
    my $config  =
    {
        db_type  => $self->prompt( 'Database type ',       'SQLite'   ),
        user     => $self->prompt( 'Database user: ',      'root'     ),
        password => $self->prompt( 'Database password: ',  's3kr1+'   ),
        db_name  => $self->prompt( 'Database name: ',      'app_data' ),
        test_db  => $self->prompt( 'Test database name: ', 'test_db'  ),
    };
    $self->notes( db_config    => $config );

    mkpath( catdir( qw( lib My App ) ) );
```

By storing this module in build_lib/, the normal build process will not install it as it does modules in lib/.

```perl
    my $dd        = Data::Dumper->new( [ $config ], [ 'db_config' ] );
    my $path      = catfile(qw( lib My App Config.pm ));

    open( my $file, '>', $path ) or die "Cannot write to '$path': $!\n";

    printf $file <<'END_HERE', $dd->Dump();
package My::App::Config;

my $db_config;
%s

sub config
{
    my ($self, $key) = @_;
    return $db_config->{$key} if exists $db_config->{$key};
}

1;
END_HERE
}

sub create_database
{
    my ($self, $dbname) = @_;
    my $config        = $self->notes( 'db_config' );
    my $dbpath        = catfile( 't', $dbname );

    local $/          = ";\n";
    local @ARGV       = catfile(qw( sql schema.sql ));
    my @sql           = <>;

    my $dbh           = DBI->connect(
        "DBI:$config->{db_type}:dbname=$dbpath",
        @$config{qw( user password )}
    );
    $dbh->do( $_ ) for @sql;
}

sub ACTION_build
{
    my $self   = shift;
    my $config = $self->notes( 'db_config' );
    $self->create_database( $config->{db_name} );
    $self->SUPER::ACTION_build( @_ );
}

sub ACTION_test
{
    my $self   = shift;
    my $config = $self->notes( 'db_config' );
    $self->create_database( $config->{test_db} );
    $self->SUPER::ACTION_test( @_ );
}

1;
```

Save the following file to *Build.PL*:

```perl
#!perl

use strict;
use warnings;

use lib 'build_lib';
use MyBuild;

my $build = MyBuild->new(
    module_name    => 'My::App',
    requires       =>
    {
        'DBI'        => '',
        'DBD::SQLite' => '',
    },
    build_requires =>
    {
        'Test::Simple' => '',
    },
);

$build->create_config_file();
$build->create_build_script();
```

Now run *Build.PL*:

```
$ perl Build.PL
Database type  [SQLite]
SQLite
Database user:  [root]
root
Database password:  [s3kr1+]
s3kr1+
Database name:  [app_data]
app_data
Test database name:  [test_db]
test_db
Deleting Build
Removed previous script 'Build'
Creating new 'Build' script for 'My-App' version '1.00'
```

Then build and test the module as usual:

```
$ perl Build
Created database 'app_data'
lib/My/App/Config.pm -> blib/lib/My/App/Config.pm
lib/My/App.pm -> blib/lib/My/App.pm
```

There aren't any tests yet, so save the following as *t/myapp.t*:

```perl
#!perl

BEGIN
{
    chdir 't' if -d 't';
}
```

```
use strict;
use warnings;

use Test::More 'no_plan'; # tests => 1;

use DBI;
use My::App::Config;

my $user    = My::App::Config->config( 'user'     );
my $pass    = My::App::Config->config( 'password' );
my $db_name = My::App::Config->config( 'test_db'  );
my $db_type = My::App::Config->config( 'db_type'  );

my $dbh     = DBI->connect( "DBI:$db_type:dbname=$db_name", $user, $pass );

my $module  = 'My::App';
use_ok( $module ) or exit;
```

SQLite
databases don't
really use
usernames and
passwords, but
play along.

Run the (simple) test:

```
$ perl Build test
Created database 'test_db'
t/myapp....ok
All tests successful.
Files=1, Tests=1,  0 wallclock secs ( 0.20 cusr +  0.00 csys =  0.20 CPU)
```

What just happened?

The initial build asked a few questions about the destination database before creating *Build.PL*. The MyBuild::create_config_file() method handles this, prompting for input while specifying sane defaults. If the user presses Enter or runs the program from an automated session such as a CPAN or a CPANPLUS shell, the program will accept the defaults.

More importantly, this also created a new file, *lib/My/App/Config.pm*. That's why running perl Build copied it into *blib/*.

How would you
delete the test
database after
running the tests?

Both perl Build and perl Build test created databases, as seen in the Created database... output. This is the purpose of the MyBuild:: ACTION_build() and MyBuild::ACTION_test() methods, which create the database with the appropriate name from the configuration data. The former builds the production database and the latter the testing database. If the user only runs perl Build, the program will not create the test database. It will create the test database only if the user runs the tests through perl Build test.

MyBuild::create_database() resembles the SQL handler seen earlier in "Shipping Test Databases."

At the end of the program, the test file loads My::App::Config as a regular module and calls its config() method to retrieve information about the testing database. Then it creates a new `DBI` connection for that database, and it can run any tests that it wants.

What about...

Q: *What if the test runs somewhere without permission to create databases?*

A: That's a problem; the best you can do is to bail out early with a decent error message and suggestions to install things manually. You *can* run parts of your test suite if you haven't managed to create the test database; some tests are better than none.

Q: *Is it a good idea to use fake data in the test database?*

A: The further your test environment is from the live environment, the more difficult it is to have confidence that you've tested the right things. You may have genuine privacy or practicality concerns, especially if you have a huge dataset or if your test data includes confidential information. For the sake of speed and simplicity, consider testing a subset of the live data, but be sure to include edge cases and oddities that you expect to encounter.

Mocking Databases

Any serious code that interacts with external libraries or programs has to deal with errors. In the case of database code, this is even more important. What happens when the database goes away? If your program crashes, you could lose valuable data.

Because error checking is so important, it's well worth testing. Yet none of the techniques shown so far make it easy to simulate database failures. Fortunately, there's one more trick: mock your database.

How do I do that?

`InsertWrapper` is a simple module that logs database connections and inserts, perhaps for diagnostics or an audit trail while developing. If it cannot connect to a database—or if the database connection goes away mysteriously—it cannot do its work, so it throws exceptions for the invoking code to handle.

Save the following example in your library directory as *InsertWrapper.pm*:

```
package InsertWrapper;

use strict;
```

```perl
use warnings;

use DBI;

sub new
{
    my ($class, %args) = @_;
    my $dbh            = DBI->connect(
        @args{qw( dsn user password )},
        { RaiseError => 1, PrintError => 0 }
    );

    my $self = bless { dbh => $dbh, logfh => $args{logfh} }, $class;
    $self->log( 'CONNECT', dsn => $args{dsn} );
    return $self;
}

sub dbh
{
    my $self = shift;
    return $self->{dbh};
}

sub log
{
    my ($self, $type, %args) = @_;
    my $logfh                = $self->{logfh};

    printf {$logfh} "[%s] %s\n", scalar( localtime() ), $type;

    while (my ($column, $value) = each %args)
    {
        printf {$logfh} "\t%s => %s\n", $column, $value;
    }
}

sub insert
{
    my ($self, $table, %args) = @_;
    my $dbh                   = $self->dbh();
    my $columns               = join(', ', keys %args);
    my $placeholders          = join(', ', ('?') x values %args);
    my $sth                   = $dbh->prepare(
        "INSERT INTO $table ($columns) VALUES ($placeholders)"
    );

    $sth->execute( values %args );
    $self->log( INSERT => %args );
}

1;
```

The important tests are that connect( ) and insert( ) do the right thing when the database is present as well as when it is absent, and that they log the appropriate messages when the database calls succeed. Save the following code as *insert_wrapper.t*:

```perl
#!perl

use strict;
use warnings;

use IO::Scalar;

use Test::More tests => 15;
use DBD::Mock;
use Test::Exception;

my $module      = 'InsertWrapper';
use_ok( $module ) or exit;

my $log_message = '';
my $fh          = IO::Scalar->new( \$log_message );
my $drh         = DBI->install_driver( 'Mock' );

can_ok( $module, 'new' );

$drh->{mock_connect_fail} = 1;

my %args = ( dsn => 'dbi:Mock:', logfh => $fh, user => '', password => '' );
throws_ok { $module->new( %args ) } qr/Could not connect/,
    'new() should fail if DB connection fails';

$drh->{mock_connect_fail} = 0;
my $wrap;
lives_ok { $wrap = $module->new( %args ) }
    '... or should succeed if connection works';
isa_ok( $wrap, $module );

like( $log_message, qr/CONNECT/,              '... logging connect message' );
like( $log_message, qr/\tdsn => $args{dsn}/, '... with dsn'           );
$log_message = '';

can_ok( $module, 'dbh' );
isa_ok( $wrap->dbh(), 'DBI::db' );

can_ok( $module, 'insert' );
$wrap->dbh()->{mock_can_connect} = 0;

throws_ok { $wrap->insert( 'users', name => 'Jerry', age => 44 ) }
    qr/prepare failed/,
    'insert() should throw exception if prepare fails';

$wrap->dbh()->{mock_can_connect} = 1;
lives_ok { $wrap->insert( 'users', name => 'Jerry', age => 44 ) }
    '... but should continue if it succeeds';
```

```
    like( $log_message, qr/INSERT/,            '... logging insert message' );
    like( $log_message, qr/\tname => Jerry/, '... with inserted data'     );
    like( $log_message, qr/\tage => 44/,      '... for each column'         );
```

Then run it with *prove*:

```
$ prove insert_wrapper.t
insert_wrapper....ok
All tests successful.
Files=1, Tests=15,  0 wallclock secs ( 0.22 cusr +  0.02 csys =  0.24 CPU)
```

What just happened?

One difference between InsertWrapper and the previous examples in this chapter is that this module creates its own database connection. It's much harder to intercept the call to DBI->connect( ) without faking the module (see "Mocking Modules" in Chapter 5). Fortunately, the DBD::Mock module provides a mock object that acts as a database driver.

The test starts by setting up the testing environment and creating an IO::Scalar object that acts like a filehandle but actually writes to the $log_message variable. Then it loads DBD::Mock and tells the DBI to consider it a valid database driver.

Remember Test:: Exception? See "Testing Exceptions" in Chapter 2.

InsertWrapper::new( ) connects to the database, if possible, setting the RaiseError flag to true. If the connection fails, DBI will throw an exception. The constructor doesn't handle this, so any exception thrown will propagate to the calling code.

To simulate a connection failure, the test sets the mock_connection_fail flag on the driver returned from the install_driver( ) code. This flag controls the connection status of every DBD::Mock object created after it; any call to DBI->connect( ) using DBD::Mock will fail.

The test also clears $log_message because subsequent prints will append to— not override—its value.

new( ) needs only one failure to prove its point, so the test then disables the connection failures by returning the flag to zero. At that point, with the connection succeeding, the code should log a success message and the connection parameters. The test checks those too.

That leaves forcing failures for InsertWrapper::insert( ). The driver-wide flag has no effect on these variables, so the test grabs the database handle of the InsertWrapper object and sets its individual mock_can_connect flag to false. DBD::Mock consults this before handling any prepare( ) or execute( ) calls, so it's the perfect way to pretend that the database connection has gone away.

As before, it takes only one test to ensure that the failures propagate to the calling code correctly. After the failure, the test code reenables the connection flag and calls insert( ) again. This time, because the state-ments should succeed, the test then checks the logged information.

What about...

Q: *Would it work to override* DBI::connect( ) *to force failures manually?*

A: Yes! There's nothing DBD::Mock does that you can't emulate with techniques shown earlier. However, the convenience of not having to write that code yourself is a big benefit.

Q: *Can you set the results of queries with* DBD::Mock?

A: Absolutely. The module has more power than shown here, including the ability to return predefined results for specific queries. Whether you prefer that or shipping a simple test database is a matter of taste. With practice, you'll understand which parts of your code need which types of tests.

Q: *What's the difference between* DBD::Mock *and* Test::MockDBI?

A: Both modules do similar things from different angles. Test::MockDBI is better when you want very fine-grained control over which state-ments succeed and which fail. It's also more complicated to learn and to use. However, it works wonderfully as a development tool for tracing the database calls, especially if you generate your SQL.

Perl.com has an introduction to Test::MockDBI at *http://www.perl. com/pub/a/2005/03/31/lightning2.html?page=2#mockdbi* and a more complete tutorial at *http://www.perl.com/pub/a/2005/07/21/ test_mockdbi.html.*

## CHAPTER 7

Testing Web Sites

Are you designing a web site and creating tests before or during its construction? Do you already have a site and want to prove that it works? A variety of design choices can help you make more robust web-based applications, from isolating the logic behind the pages to ensuring what happens when a user clicks the Submit button. The CPAN provides several modules that allow you to create useful tests for your web applications.

This chapter demonstrates how to build web applications with testing in mind as well as how to test them when you deploy them. The labs show how to record your interaction with these programs and how to validate HTML in a few different ways. Finally, the chapter walks through setting up an instance of the Apache web server specifically designed to make testing Apache modules easy.

Testing Your Backend

A friend of one of the authors has frequent table tennis tournaments at his workplace and has long considered building a web application to keep track of player rankings. The application, Scorekeeper, should maintain a list of games, who played in each game, the final scores for each game, and when the game took place. The application also should show how well players perform against others overall—mostly for heckling purposes.

The conceptual relationships are immediately apparent: a game has two scores and each score has a player and a game. It's easy to model this with a relational database. The next step is to build the GUI, right?

Your 1,500-line
single-file program
works, but can you
prove it?

Suppose that you write this application in the unfortunate style of many CGI programs in Perl's history. It's 1,500 lines long, and it contains giant conditional blocks or maybe something resembling a dispatch table. It might contain raw SQL statements, or it might use some kind of hand-rolled database abstraction. How hard is it to add a ladder system or add play-by-play recording? What if your friend suddenly wants a command-line client or a GTK interface?

To make this program easier to extend and test, separate the backend database interaction, the display of the data, and the logic needed to control them. This pattern, sometimes referred to as Model-View-Controller, allows you to test your code more easily and leads to better code organization and reuse.

How do I do that?

The introduction described the relationships of the application, so the database structure is straightforward: every game, score, and player has a table. Each game has scores, and each score has a player associated with it. This lab uses SQLite, which provides a fully functional SQL database without running a server. Save the following SQL as *schema.sql*:

```
BEGIN TRANSACTION;
CREATE TABLE game (
    id   INTEGER PRIMARY KEY,
    date INTEGER
);
CREATE TABLE score (
    id     INTEGER PRIMARY KEY,
    game   INTEGER,
    player INTEGER,
    value  INTEGER
);
CREATE TABLE player (
    id   INTEGER PRIMARY KEY,
    name TEXT UNIQUE
);
COMMIT;
```

If you need to
start with an
empty database,
remove the
keeper.db file
and rerun the
sqlite command.

Now, pipe the SQL file to the sqlite command, providing the path to the database file as the first argument:

```
$ sqlite keeper.db < schema.sql
```

You now have an empty SQLite database stored in *keeper.db*, and you can work with it using the *sqlite* utility. The rest of this lab uses only Perl modules to manipulate the Scorekeeper data. Save the following code as *player.t*:

```perl
use Test::More tests => 18;
use Test::Exception;
use Test::Deep;

use strict;
use warnings;

BEGIN
{
    use_ok('Scorekeeper');
}

my $a = Scorekeeper::Player->create( { name => 'PlayerA' } );
my $b = Scorekeeper::Player->create( { name => 'PlayerB' } );
my $c = Scorekeeper::Player->create( { name => 'PlayerC' } );

END
{
    foreach my $player ( $a, $b, $c )
    {
        $player->games->delete_all();
        $player->delete();
    }
}

dies_ok { Scorekeeper::Player->create( { name -> $a->name() } ) }
    'cannot create two players with the same name';

foreach my $tuple ( [ 11, 8 ], [ 9, 11 ], [ 11, 7 ], [ 10, 11 ], [ 11, 9 ] )
{
    my ( $score1, $score2 ) = @$tuple;

    my $g = Scorekeeper::Game->create( {} );
    $g->add_to_scores( { player => $a, value => $score1 } );
    $g->add_to_scores( { player => $b, value => $score2 } );
}

my $g2 = Scorekeeper::Game->create( {} );
$g2->add_to_scores( { player => $a, value => 11 } );
$g2->add_to_scores( { player => $c, value => 8 } );

is( scalar( $a->games() ), 6 );
is( scalar( $b->games() ), 5 );

is( $a->wins(),    4, "player A's wins"   );
is( $b->wins(),    2, "player B's wins"   );
is( $c->wins(),    0, "player C's wins"   );

is( $a->losses(), 2, "player A's losses" );
is( $b->losses(), 3, "player B's losses" );
is( $c->losses(), 1, "player C's losses" );
```

```
    cmp_deeply( [ $a->opponents() ], bag( $b, $c ), "player A's opponents" );
    is_deeply(  [ $b->opponents() ], [$a],          "player B's opponents" );
    is_deeply(  [ $c->opponents() ], [$a],          "player C's opponents" );

    is( $a->winning_percentage_against($b), 60,  'A vs B' );
    is( $b->winning_percentage_against($a), 40,  'B vs A' );

    is( $a->winning_percentage_against($c), 100, 'A vs C' );
    is( $c->winning_percentage_against($a), 0,   'C vs A' );

    is_deeply(
        [ Scorekeeper::Player->retrieve_all_ranked() ],
        [ $a, $b, $c ],
        'players retrieved in the correct order of rank'
    );
```

One of Class::DBI's many extensions is Class::DBI::Loader, which uses table and field names from the database to set up Class::DBI classes automatically. Another is Class::DBI::Loader::Relationship, which allows you to describe database relations as simple English sentences. The Scorekeeper module uses these modules to initialize classes for the database schema. Save the following as *Scorekeeper.pm*:

```
package Scorekeeper;

use strict;
use warnings;

use Class::DBI::Loader;
use Class::DBI::Loader::Relationship;

my $loader = Class::DBI::Loader->new(
    dsn       => 'dbi:SQLite2:dbname=keeper.db',
    namespace => 'Scorekeeper',
);

$loader->relationship( 'a game has scores'               );
$loader->relationship( 'a player has games with scores' );

package Scorekeeper::Game;

sub is_winner
{
    my ( $self, $player ) = @_;

    my @scores =
        sort {
            return 0 unless $a and $b;
            $b->value() <=> $a->value()
        }
        $self->scores();
    return $player eq $scores[0]->player();
}
```

```perl
sub has_player
{
    my ( $self, $player ) = @_;

    ( $player == $_->player() ) && return 1 for $self->scores();
    return 0;
}

package Scorekeeper::Player;

sub wins
{
    my ($self) = @_;
    return scalar grep { $_->is_winner($self) } $self->games();
}

sub losses
{
    my ($self) = @_;
    return scalar( $self->games() ) - $self->wins();
}

sub winning_percentage_against
{
    my ( $self, $other ) = @_;

    my @all = grep { $_->has_player($other) } $self->games();
    my @won = grep { $_->is_winner($self) } @all;

    return @won / @all * 100;
}

sub retrieve_all_ranked
{
    my ($self) = @_;
    return sort { $b->wins() <=> $a->wins() }
        $self->retrieve_all();
}

sub opponents
{
    my ($self) = @_;

    my %seen;
    $seen{$_}++ for map { $_->player() } map { $_->scores() }
        $self->games();
    delete $seen{$self};

    return grep { exists $seen{$_} } $self->retrieve_all();
}

1;
```

Replacing the "return if true for any" idiom in has_player() with the List::MoreUtils::any() function will make the code much clearer. That module has many other wonderful functions, too.

Now run *player.t* with *prove*. All of the tests should pass:

```
$ prove player.t
player....ok
All tests successful.
Files=1, Tests=18,  1 wallclock secs ( 0.68 cusr +  0.08 csys =  0.76 CPU)
```

What just happened?

If you've written database code before, you may have spent a lot of time storing and retrieving data from various tables. If only there were a really slick way to turn these relationships into Perl classes without ever writing a single SQL statement! There are, in fact, a handful of modules that do just that, including Class::DBI. If you're not familiar with Class::DBI, this test file demonstrates how little code it takes to set up these relationships.

By default, deleting a Class:: DBI object also deletes its immediate relations.

When testing databases, it's a good idea to clean up any data left over after the tests end. To do this, the test file declares an END block containing statements to execute when the program ends, even if it dies. The END block iterates through every new player created and deletes any games and scores associated with that player and then the player itself, leaving no extra records in the database. (See "Testing Database Data" in Chapter 6 for more.)

The database schema specified that a player's name must be unique. To test this constraint, *player.t* attempts to create a fourth player in a dies_ok( ) block with the same name as player $a. If creating the player fails, as it should, dies_ok( ) will report a success.

After adding some fake scores, *player.t* performs a couple of tests to see if the games( ), wins( ), losses( ), and winning_percentage_against( ) methods return accurate values. The most interesting test uses Test:: Deep's cmp_deeply( ) to verify the opponents of $a are indeed the two other players that $a has played.

cmp_deeply( ) and bag( ) can check the contents of an array without knowing the order of the items it contains.

The backend for Scorekeeper now has decent test coverage. You can be confident that any graphical view that you create for the Scorekeeper data will display accurate information.

Testing Your Frontend

Once you've fully tested the backend of your web application, you should test its frontend as well. Assume that you have expanded the Scorekeeper application (see "Testing Your Backend," earlier in this chapter) to contain interfaces for adding players and games. The steps for testing by hand are straightforward: open the application in the browser, type things into the form fields, click Submit, and check the contents of the resulting page. Then repeat. Unfortunately, as the application grows, so does the punch list of manual regression tests you need to perform to make sure everything works.

This lab shows how to automate the testing of web applications using Test::WWW::Mechanize, a subclass of WWW::Mechanize that works well for test programs.

How do I do that?

This lab tests the frontend of the CPAN Search site (*http://search.cpan.org/*). This web site has one primary form that allows users to find modules as well as some navigational links to take visitors to the most-frequented parts of the site.

When constructing tests for web applications, always start by listing the behavior you expect from the application. How do you expect the CPAN Search Site to work?

You could use similar code to test the frontend of the Scorekeeper application.

- I should be able to retrieve the CPAN Search Site home page successfully.
- If I search the modules for "frobnicate", there shouldn't be any results.
- If I search the modules for "test", there should be many results.
- Once I've searched for "test", all of the links on the resulting page should work.

These assertions sound pretty solid. Save the following file as *mech.t*:

```perl
#!perl

use strict;
use warnings;

use Test::More tests => 6;
use Test::WWW::Mechanize;

my $mech = Test::WWW::Mechanize->new();

$mech->get_ok( 'http://search.cpan.org/' );

$mech->title_is( 'search.cpan.org: The CPAN Search Site' );

$mech->form_name( 'f' );
$mech->field( 'query', 'frobnicate' );
$mech->select( 'mode', 'module'      );
```

```
$mech->submit( );

$mech->content_contains( 'No matches' );

$mech->back( );

$mech->field( 'query', 'test' );
$mech->submit( );

$mech->content_like( qr/ Results .+ Found /sx );
$mech->content_lacks( 'No matches' );
$mech->page_links_ok( );
```

Running *mech.t* should result in six successful tests. The last test may take a bit longer than the first five, depending on the speed of your network connection.

What just happened?

After useing the Test::WWW::Mechanize module, the test file creates an object of that class, $mech. The $mech object pretends to be a real human that fills in forms and clicks on links and buttons. It even keeps a history, meaning that the back( ) method works just like the Back button in your favorite browser.

WWW::Mechanize provides other methods to fill out and submit a form in one statement.

The first step is to instruct $mech to retrieve the CPAN Search home page, which contains a single form named simply f. The get_ok( ) method not only does this, but also reports a successful test if it fetched the web page without an error.

Next, $mech checks the title of the fetch page. title_is( ) ensures that the title is exactly the string specified. Test::WWW::Mechanize also provides alternative title_like( ) and title_unlike( ) methods that check whether the title matches or does not match a given regular expression.

Many of the other methods on Test::WWW::Mechanize objects have is( )/isnt( ) or like( )/unlike( ) variants. See the Test::WWW::Mechanize module documentation for details.

The test selects the form named f as the form for which to specify input values. $mech then simulates filling out the text field named query and selecting the item from the pop-up menu named mode with the value of module. The submit( ) method then "clicks" the Submit button for the form, and the $mech object happily retrieves the resulting page.

At the time of this writing, there aren't any modules with names containing the word "frobnicate," thus the search results should be empty. $mech ensures that the resulting page contains the phrase "No matches" by using the content_contains( ) method.

$mech next clicks its virtual Back button and jumps back to the page containing the original web form. Because the object has already selected the correct pop-up menu item in the form, $mech only needs to change the text field to contain "test." It then submits the form again.

This time, there are lots of modules with the word "test" in their names. The test checks that the results page *does not* contain the phrase "No matches" as seen earlier.

Test::WWW::Mechanize provides a convenience function, page_links_ok( ), to test that it can follow all of the links on the current page successfully. Because there are more than 50 links on the results page, and Mechanize retrieves each one, this takes a little while. If all of the links are indeed valid, page_links_ok( ) produces a sixth successful test.

Record and Play Back Browsing Sessions

Creating lengthy programs to test web applications might seem a bit tedious. The *mech-dump* utility that comes with WWW::Mechanize prints the names and elements of every form and provides some relief when searching for form and form element names. However, using that data in your tests means that you'll have to cut and paste multiple small blocks of code. Yuck.

Relieve some of the hassle by using HTTP::Recorder to set up an HTTP proxy to record the pages you visit and the forms you fill out. As you browse, HTTP::Recorder saves each action as WWW::Mechanize code.

> The mech-dump utility that comes with WWW:: Mechanize prints out everything that a WWW:: Mechanize object knows about a web page.

How do I do that?

Save the following listing as *recorder.pl*:

```perl
#!perl

use strict;
use warnings;

use HTTP::Recorder;
use HTTP::Proxy;

my $agent = HTTP::Recorder->new( file => "mech2.t", showwindow => 1 );

my $proxy = HTTP::Proxy->new(
   port  => 4567,
   agent => $agent,
```

> At the time of this writing, HTTP::Recorder is incomplete, though it's still worth using as a base from which you can develop test files for web interaction.

```
    );

    $proxy->start();
```

Next, configure your browser's proxy settings to connect to your own machine as a proxy on port 4567, as Figure 7-1 shows. Don't forget to restore the original settings after you finish this lab!

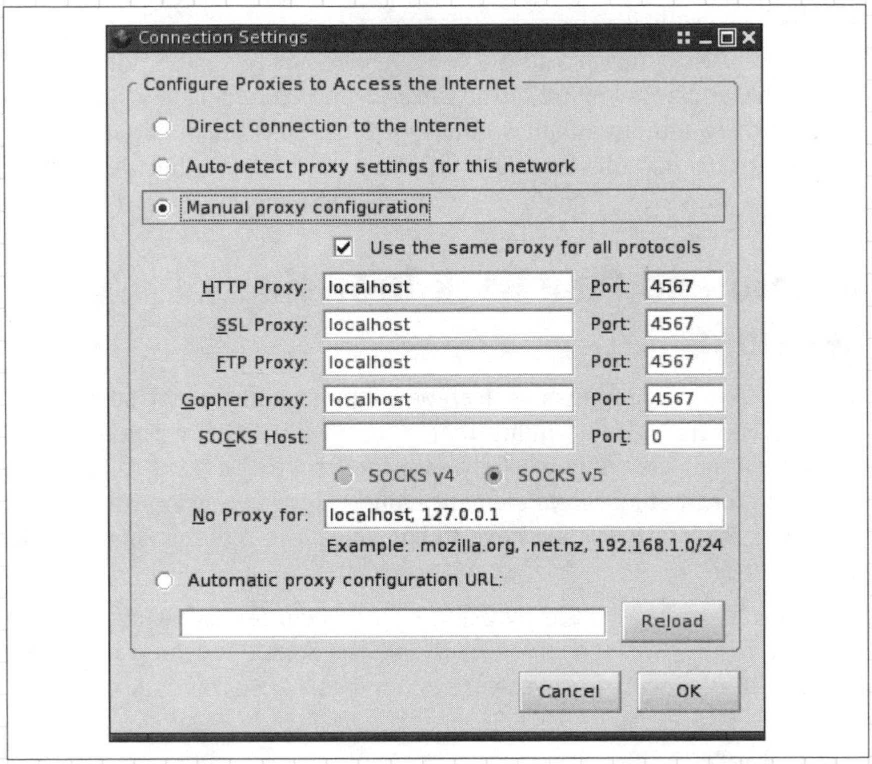

Figure 7-1. Proxy connection settings in Mozilla Firefox

Now run *recorder.pl*. You won't see any output from the program while it's running, so don't hold your breath.

```
$ perl recorder.pl
```

Go to *http://search.cpan.org/* in your browser. If everything went as planned, you'll see a pop-up window appear with Perl code!

Search the CPAN for "gerbil counting" and click the Submit button, and then click on the Home link at the top. Search for something else and click Next once a page of results appears. As you're doing this, the pop-up window will refresh with every request to show updated Perl code. Figure 7-2 shows an example.

Using Mozilla Firefox or some other pop-up-blocking tool? Allow pop-ups while you're doing this lab to see HTTP::Recorder's window.

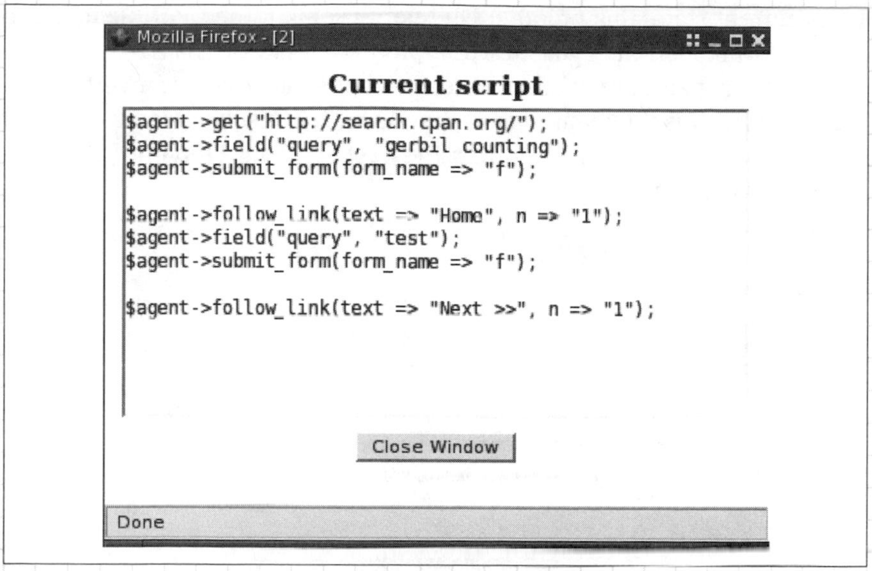

Figure 7-2. Pop-up window produced by HTTP::Recorder

What just happened?

Running *recorder.pl* starts an HTTP proxy daemon that your browser uses to make requests. The proxy uses an HTTP::Recorder agent, which attempts to keep track of submitted forms and log the requests in the form of Perl code. It saves a logfile as *mech2.t*, which you specifed when creating the HTTP::Recorder object. Additionally, because showwindow is true, the proxy modifies the content of the requested page to display a pop-up window with the current contents of *mech2.t*.

The Perl code saved to *mech2.t* is actually a series of statements involving a hypothetical WWW::Mechanize object. You can add the object yourself:

```perl
#!perl

use WWW::Mechanize;

my $agent = WWW::Mechanize->new( autocheck => 1 );

$agent->get("http://search.cpan.org/");
$agent->field("query", "gerbil counting");
$agent->submit_form(form_name => "f");

$agent->follow_link(text => "Home", n => "1");
$agent->field("query", "test");
$agent->submit_form(form_name => "f");

$agent->follow_link(text => "Next >>", n => "1");
```

In its current state, this program isn't very useful. If the CPAN Search Site ceases to function and you run this program, WWW::Mechanize won't be able to fill out the forms and will die. A better idea is to convert it to a test file, which is why you named the file with a *.t* suffix. Modify *mech2.t* to use Test::WWW::Mechanize (from the "Testing Your Frontend" lab, earlier in this chapter):

```perl
#!perl

use strict;

use Test::More tests => 3;
use Test::WWW::Mechanize;

my $agent = Test::WWW::Mechanize->new;

$agent->get_ok( 'http://search.cpan.org/' );
$agent->field( 'query', 'gerbil counting' );
$agent->submit_form( form_name => 'f' );

$agent->follow_link_ok( { text => 'Home', n => '1' } );
$agent->field( 'query', 'test' );
$agent->submit_form( form_name => 'f' );

$agent->follow_link_ok( { text => 'Next >>', n => '1' } );
```

Running the modified *mech2.t* should produce three passing tests.

To turn the HTTP::Recorder output into tests, the code instantiates $agent as a Test::WWW::Mechanize object. Note that statements that work as tests have changed. When defining $agent, the test file doesn't need autocheck => 1 any more because it uses get_ok( ) and follow_link_ok( ) to test the success of a request. follow_link_ok( ) expects a hash reference of arguments just as follow_link( ) does.

Testing the Validity of HTML

As you test the features of your web applications, you also may want to make sure the HTML content that your code produces conforms to the standards set by the World Wide Web Consortium (*http://www.w3.org/*). Coding to standards makes your site cleaner, easier to maintain, and more accessible from a variety of browsers and clients, especially for users with disabilities.

How do I do that?

The Test::HTML::Tidy module provides a single function, html_tidy_ok( ), that checks the completeness and correctness of an HTML document. Save the following code as *tidy.t*:

```perl
#!perl

use strict;

use Test::More tests => 2;
use Test::WWW::Mechanize;
use Test::HTML::Tidy;

my $mech = Test::WWW::Mechanize->new( );

$mech->get_ok( 'http://search.cpan.org/' );

html_tidy_ok( $mech->content );

$mech->field( 'query', 'otter spotting' );
$mech->submit( );

html_tidy_ok( $mech->content( ) );
```

When running the test file, you may see successes or failures, depending on the current conformity of the CPAN Search Site.

You might already be familiar with the tidy command. Test:: HTML::Tidy uses HTML::Tidy as a backend, which in turn uses the tidy library.

What just happened?

tidy.t uses Test::HTML::Tidy along with Test::WWW::Mechanize to make sure the CPAN Search Site's home page is valid HTML. The first test passes the entire HTML document, $mech->content, to html_tidy_ok( ), which reports success if the page validates. The test then searches the CPAN for "otter spotting" and checks the HTML of the resulting page as well.

What about...

Q: *Can I check a smaller portion of HTML instead of an entire document?*

A: Use Test::HTML::Lint, which exports an html_ok( ) function to which you can pass any bit of HTML. Save the following listing as *table.t*:

```perl
#!perl

use strict;
```

Test::HTML::Lint uses HTML::Lint as a backend.

```
use Test::More tests => 1;
use Test::HTML::Lint;

html_ok( <<'EOF' );

<h1>My Favorite Sciuridae</h1>

<table>
    <trh>
        <td>Grey squirrel</td>
        <td>plump, calm</td>
    </tr>
    <tr>
        <td>Red squirrel</td>
        <td>quick, shifty</td>
    <tr>
        <td>Yellow-bellied Marmot</td>
        <td>aloof</td>
    </tr>
</table>

EOF
```

Yep, those errors are intentional.

Run the test file with *prove*:

```
$ prove -v part.t
part....1..1
not ok 1
#       Failed test (part.t at line 8)
# Errors:
#   (5:5) Unknown element <trh>
#   (8:5) </tr> with no opening <tr>
#   (16:1) <trh> at (5:5) is never closed
#   (16:1) <tr> at (9:5) is never closed
# Looks like you failed 1 tests of 1.
dubious
    Test returned status 1 (wstat 256, 0x100)
DIED. FAILED test 1
    Failed 1/1 tests, 0.00% okay
Failed 1/1 test scripts, 0.00% okay. 1/1 subtests failed, 0.00% okay.
Failed Test Stat Wstat Total Fail  Failed  List of Failed
-------------------------------------------------------------------------
part.t          1   256     1     1 100.00%  1
```

html_ok( ) reports the single test as a failure and reports exactly where the document has errors. The error reports take the form of (*line number : character position*), where the line number is the line number of the provided HTML. As the output explains, Test:: HTML::Lint has no idea what a <trh> tag is. Nevertheless, neither it nor the <tr> tag ever close. There's more work to do before putting this table of favorite furry animals online.

Running Your Own Apache Server

Testing web applications or Apache modules might be as easy as testing the web applications in previous labs: configure Apache, run the server, and then run the tests. However, it can become a pain to make sure the Apache server is in a pristine state every time you want to run the tests. Apache-Test gives you the ability to start and stop a special Apache server to use for automated testing of Apache modules.

Apache-Test is the distribution that contains Apache::Test and the related modules.

How do I do that?

Apache-Test needs a *t/* directory for the server configuration, document root, and test files. Create the directories *lib/*, *t/*, and *t/conf/*.

You also need a tiny program to start and stop the Apache server as well as to run the tests. Save the following as *t/TEST*:

```perl
#!perl

use strict;

use Apache::TestRun;
Apache::TestRun->new->run(@ARGV);
```

Suppose that you want to serve your photo album from the test server, a step that requires adding custom directives to Apache's configuration. Save the following as *t/conf/extra.conf.in*:

You need to adjust the second argument of Alias to the full path of the directory you want to serve.

```
Alias /pictures /home/anu/pictures

<Location /pictures>
    Options +Indexes
    Allow from all
</Location>
```

It's also a good idea to tell Apache-Test where your Apache executable is. Do this by setting the APACHE_TEST_HTTPD environment variable in your shell:

```
$ export APACHE_TEST_HTTPD=/usr/sbin/apache-perl
```

Now, run *TEST* with the -start-httpd argument to start the demo server on the default Apache-Test port:

If you use something besides the Bourne shell or a derivative, consult the manual for instructions on setting an environment variable.

```
$ perl t/TEST -start-httpd
[warning] setting ulimit to allow core files
ulimit -c unlimited; /usr/bin/perl /home/anu/setup/t/TEST -start-httpd
/usr/sbin/apache-perl  -d /home/anu/setup/t -f
    /home/anu/setup/t/conf/httpd.conf -D APACHE1 -D PERL_USEITHREADS
using Apache/1.3.33
```

```
waiting 60 seconds for server to start: .
waiting 60 seconds for server to start: ok (waited 0 secs)
server localhost:8529 started
```

Congratulations—you now have a web server serving your photo gallery!

There are a few things to note in the output, such as which Apache executable actually ran (/usr/sbin/apache-perl). The output also shows two options passed to the executable, the server root (-d /home/anu/setup/t) and the configuration file it used (-f /home/anu/setup/t/conf/httpd.conf). The output displays what version of Apache is in use, and then a few lines while the server starts. Finally, the last line of the output shows the host and port the daemon uses.

Navigate to the host and port with your browser. You should be able to browse the directory you specified in *extra.conf.in*, as Figure 7-3 shows.

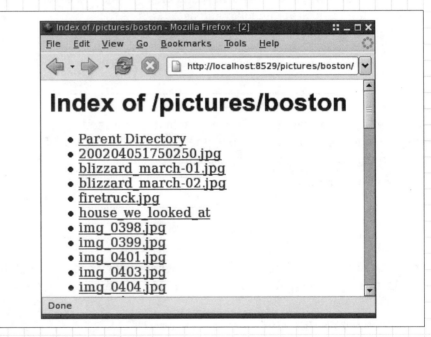

Figure 7-3. Using a test Apache server

When you finish browsing and want to shut down the server, run *TEST* with the -stop-httpd argument:

```
$ perl t/TEST -stop-httpd
[warning] setting ulimit to allow core files
ulimit -c unlimited; /usr/bin/perl /home/anu/setup/t/TEST -stop-httpd
[warning] server localhost:8529 shutdown
```

You should no longer be able to access the web server with your browser.

What just happened?

The *TEST* program puts together all of the pieces to execute and manage an Apache server and test suite that uses it. When you run *TEST*, it creates a configuration file that incorporates any additional files you provide, such as *conf/extra.conf.in*. *TEST* also creates a logging directory, *t/logs/* by default, which holds the standard *access_log* and *error_log* files. After initialization, *TEST* launches an Apache server that listens on port 8529 by default.

TEST has many command-line options such as -verbose, which shows many more diagnostics. You can also use the -clean option to remove the slew of autogenerated files Apache-Test creates when it starts the server. Run TEST -help for a complete list of options.

Testing with Apache-Test

"Running Your Own Apache Server" demonstrated how to start and stop an Apache server manually. In real life, you'll probably start and stop the test server automatically when you want to run your test suite. This lab shows how to test and create a simple Apache module, called Thumbnail, that uses the Imager module to resize images to a certain width and height. How do you know this module works? Use Apache-Test to test it!

How do I do that?

First, create a *lib/* directory. You should already have the *t/* and */t/conf/* directories from the previous lab. *t/TEST* will be the same, but *t/conf/ extra.conf.in* needs some editing.

In custom configuration files such as *extra.conf.in*, the server substitutes special variables (in the form of @*NAME*@) with useful values when it starts. The server uses those directives in the file as its configuration. Adding the *lib/* directory to Perl's module search path is easy; add it to the SERVERROOT variable.

Remember to add this new lib/ directory to Perl's search path.

Save the following as *t/conf/extra.conf.in*:

```
<IfModule mod_perl.c>

    <Perl>
        use lib '@SERVERROOT@/../lib';
        use Thumbnail ();
    </Perl>

    <Location /images>
        SetHandler perl-script
```

```
          PerlHandler Thumbnail
      </Location>

    </IfModule>
```

Save the Thumbnail module as *lib/Thumbnail.pm*:

```perl
package Thumbnail;

use strict;
use warnings;

use Apache::Constants qw(:common);
use Apache::File;
use Imager;

our $constraint = 150;

sub handler
{
    my ($r) = @_;

    return DECLINED unless $r->content_type() =~ m{^image/};

    my $img = Imager->new();
    $img->open( file => $r->filename ) or die $img->errstr();

    $img    = $img->scale( xpixels => $constraint, ypixels => $constraint );

    my ( $tmpfile, $tmpfh ) = Apache::File->tmpfile();
    $img->write( file => $tmpfile, type => 'jpeg' )
        or die $img->errstr();

    $r->send_http_header('image/jpeg');
    $r->send_fd($tmpfh);

    return OK;
}

1;
```

Save the following test file as *t/thumbnail.t*:

```perl
#!perl

use strict;
use warnings;

use Apache::Test;
use Apache::TestUtil;
use Apache::TestRequest qw( GET_BODY );
use Imager;

plan( tests => 1, need_module('mod_perl') );
```

```
my $content = GET_BODY('/images/panorama.jpg');

my $img     = Imager->new();
$img->open( data => $content, type => 'jpeg' )
    or die $img->errstr();

my $max     = 150;

t_debug( "assuming constraint is $max pixels" );

t_debug( 'width: '  . $img->getwidth()   );
t_debug( 'height: ' . $img->getheight()  );

ok( ( $img->getwidth() == $max ) or ( $img->getheight() == $max ) );
```

Finally, you need a picture for the module to transform. Pick something large, such as a breathtaking scene of Bryce Canyon with deer grazing in the distance. Save it as *t/htdocs/images/panorama.jpg*.

First make sure that Apache-Test knows where to find your Apache executable by setting the APACHE_TEST_HTTPD environment variable:

```
$ export APACHE_TEST_HTTPD=/usr/sbin/apache-perl
```

Run *TEST* to run the tests:

```
$ perl t/TEST
[warning] setting ulimit to allow core files
ulimit -c unlimited; /usr/bin/perl /home/anu/thumbnail/t/TEST
/usr/sbin/apache-perl  -d /home/anu/thumbnail/t -f
    /home/anu/thumbnail/t/conf/httpd.conf -D APACHE1 -D PERL_USEITHREADS
using Apache/1.3.33

waiting 60 seconds for server to start: .
waiting 60 seconds for server to start: ok (waited 0 secs)
server localhost:8529 started
t/thumbnail....ok
All tests successful.
Files=1, Tests=1,  2 wallclock secs ( 0.35 cusr +  0.05 csys =  0.40 CPU)
[warning] server localhost:8529 shutdown
```

If you're not using a bash-like shell, see your shell's documentation to set this variable correctly.

Within the Apache-Test diagnostic output, you'll see that all of the tests succeeded.

What just happened?

t/ is the server root directory, which is where Apache looks for the *conf/* or *htdocs/* directory. If an *htdocs/* directory is present, Apache will use it as the document root. By default, Apache-Test saves a simple *index.html* in the document root when it starts, but the *images/* directory is more interesting right now.

Requesting the URI /images/panorama.jpg without using the handler would simply return the picture of the canyon with the lovely grazing Cervidae. *extra.conf.in*, however, uses a <Location> directive to specify that the thumbnail-generating module will handle paths beginning with /images.

Thumbnail is a fairly straightforward Apache module. It handles only images, returning DECLINED if Apache doesn't believe that the file's type is some sort of image. If it *is* an image, the handler reads in the file and resizes it (in memory, not on disk) so that it is at the most 150 pixels square. Finally, it sends the resized image as the content of the response.

...or does it? Does the module truly resize the image? This is precisely what *t/thumbnail.t* tests.

thumbnail.t doesn't use Test::More. Instead, it uses Apache-Test's framework, which is a bit different. Remember, though, that tests always boil down to a simple "ok" or "not ok."

The first difference is that Apache::Test provides a different plan() function. While it appears the same as the Test::More version, it actually provides many more features, allowing developers to specify requirements for the tests that skip the tests if not met. *thumbnail.t* ensures that the Apache server used for testing does indeed have mod_perl enabled by specifying need_module('mod_perl'). Without mod_perl, the file skips the tests.

Alternatively, you can use need_module() to specify that the tests require a certain Perl module. For example, to modify the plan() statement to specify that you need the Imager module, write:

```
plan tests => 1, need_module('Imager');
```

To skip the test file completely, use the skip_reason() function exported by Apache::Test in combination with plan():

```
plan tests => 1, skip_reason("our Perl ain't up to snuff");
```

This is merely the tip of the iceberg in terms of what Apache::Test's plan() function can do. For more information, see the Apache::Test documentation.

Continuing with differences between Apache-Test and Test::More, note that there are no is() or diag() functions. Instead, Apache::TestUtil exports t_cmp() and t_debug(). t_cmp() takes the same arguments as is(), but you must use it in conjunction with ok(). For example, to test that the image uses 16-bit color:

```
ok( t_cmp($img->bits(), 16, 'image has sixteen bits') );
```

Instead of printing a gigantic scalar, Thumbnail.pm uses Apache::File to create a temporary file and uses the send_fd() method with a filehandle.

t_debug( ) prints out diagnostic messages in the same manner as Test::More's diag( ) function. *thumbnail.t* uses t_debug( ) to print out the value of the image's actual size. To see these diagnostic messages, run *TEST* with the -verbose option. When you do, you'll see other debugging information in addition to your own messages:

```
$ perl t/TEST -verbose
[warning] setting ulimit to allow core files
ulimit -c unlimited; /usr/bin/perl /home/anu/thumbnail/t/TEST -verbose
/usr/sbin/apache-perl  -d /home/anu/thumbnail/t -f
    /home/anu/thumbnail/t/conf/httpd.conf -D APACHE1 -D PERL_USEITHREADS
using Apache/1.3.33

waiting 60 seconds for server to start: .
waiting 60 seconds for server to start: ok (waited 0 secs)
server localhost:8529 started
t/thumbnail....1..1
# Running under perl version 5.008004 for linux
# Current time local: Thu Mar 24 11:13:55 2005
# Current time GMT:   Thu Mar 24 16:13:55 2005
# Using Test.pm version 1.24
# Using Apache/Test.pm version 1.20
# assuming constraint is 150 pixels
# width: 200
# height: 150
ok 1
ok
All tests successful.
Files=1, Tests=1,  1 wallclock secs ( 0.35 cusr +  0.06 csys =  0.41 CPU)
[warning] server localhost:8529 shutdown
```

The biggest step is to contact the test server to make requests so that you can test whether the returned content is what you expected. Apache::TestRequest optionally exports a slew of functions that make this easy. *thumbnail.t* uses the GET_BODY( ) function, which makes a simple GET request to the test server and returns the content. By using Apache::TestRequest's functions, you never have to know the port number or IP address of your test server.

Other useful Apache::TestRequest exports include functions such as GET( ), HEAD( ), PUT( ), and POST( ) to make those types of requests. Each of these has a corresponding _OK function. For example, GET_OK( ) makes a GET request and checks the resulting response code. Similarly, _BODY functions retrieve just the content of the response. _BODY_ASSERT functions check the success of the request *and* return the content. Finally, a set of UPLOAD( ) functions exist for sending entire files.

If your tests suddenly stop working, run TEST with the "-clean" option to remove extra generated files. Then be sure to run TEST with "-verbose".

Want even more diagnostic output? Set APACHE_TEST_TRACE_LEVEL=debug and APACHE_TEST_COLOR=1 to see colorized, lower-level debugging information.

If you extended Thumbnail.pm to allow the pixel constraint to be set in the Apache configuration with PerlSetVar, what would you add to the tests?

What about...

Q: *Can I use other test modules with* Apache::Test?

A: Sure. Provide -withtestmore as an argument to use Apache::Test and all of Test::More's functions instantly become available:

```perl
#!perl

use strict;
use warnings;

use Apache::Test qw(-withtestmore);
use Apache::TestUtil;
use Apache::TestRequest qw( GET_BODY );
use Imager;

plan( tests => 1, need_module('mod_perl') );

my $content = GET_BODY('/images/panorama.jpg');

my $img     = Imager->new();
$img->open( data => $content, type => 'jpeg' )
    or die $img->errstr();

my $max     = 150;

diag( 'assuming constraint is $max pixels' );

diag( 'width: '  . $img->getwidth()  );
diag( 'height: ' . $img->getheight() );

ok( ( $img->getwidth() == $max ) or ( $img->getheight() == $max ) );
```

Note that at the time of this writing, compatibility with test modules that use Test::Builder is still experimental.

Where to learn more

This lab is only a glimpse into the world of testing Apache with Perl. More advanced concepts include testing C modules and debugging tests. "Running and Developing Tests with the Apache::Test Framework" at *http://perl.apache.org/docs/general/testing/testing.html* covers these subjects in more detail.

Distributing Modules
with Apache-Test

The previous lab, "Testing with Apache-Test," created a simple Apache module that you tested with Apache-Test. Suppose that the module is so handy, useful, and original that you want to share it with the world. How do you set up your tests in a module distribution?

This lab demonstrates how to set up a module distribution for use with Module::Build and the Apache-Test testing framework.

How do I do that?

Keep all of the files you created from the previous lab except for *t/TEST*; Apache-Test will create it for you automatically. Save the following as *Build.PL* in the directory that contains both *t/* and *lib/*:

```perl
#!perl

use Module::Build;

my $build_pkg =
    eval { require Apache::TestMB } ? 'Apache::TestMB' : 'Module::Build';

my $build = $build_pkg->new(
    module_name  => 'Thumbnail',
    dist_version => 0.01,
    license      => 'perl',
    requires     => {
        'Apache::Test' => 1.12,
        'Imager'       => 0.40,
    },
);

$build->create_build_script();
```

Then build and test like any other Module::Build-based distribution:

```
$ perl Build.PL
Creating new 'Build' script for 'Thumbnail' version '0.01'
$ perl Build test
lib/Thumbnail.pm -> blib/lib/Thumbnail.pm
/usr/bin/perl -I /home/anu/thumbnail/blib/lib -I
    /home/anu/thumbnail/blib/arch t/TEST -clean
[warning] setting ulimit to allow core files
ulimit -c unlimited; /usr/bin/perl /home/anu/thumbnail/t/TEST -clean
/usr/bin/perl -I /home/anu/thumbnail/blib/lib -I /home/anu/thumbnail/blib/
arch
    t/TEST -bugreport -verbose=0
[warning] setting ulimit to allow core files
```

Did "Build test" fail? Check to see that Apache-Test has the correct path to the Apache executable. If it's not correct, set the APACHE_TEST_ HTTPD environment variable to what you used in the previous lab.

```
ulimit -c unlimited; /usr/bin/perl /home/anu/thumbnail/t/TEST -bugreport
    -verbose=0
/usr/sbin/apache-perl  -d /home/anu/thumbnail/t -f
    /home/anu/thumbnail/t/conf/httpd.conf -D APACHE1 -D PERL_USEITHREADS
using Apache/1.3.33

waiting 60 seconds for server to start: .
waiting 60 seconds for server to start: ok (waited 0 secs)
server localhost:8529 started
t/thumbnail.............ok
All tests successful.
Files=1, Tests=1,  4 wallclock secs ( 0.67 cusr +  0.08 csys =  0.75 CPU)
[warning] server localhost:8529 shutdown
```

Add documentation (if you haven't already) and some tweaking to *Build. PL*, and your distribution is ready to go!

What just happened?

Apache::TestMB adds Apache-Test features to Module::Build, which, among other things, automatically create a *TEST* file for you. Running perl Build test prepares the distribution and runs the test suite using *TEST*.

Users who don't have Apache-Test installed when they run perl Build. PL will see a large warning about the missing prerequisite. However, they can still build and install the distribution.

What about...

Q: *What if I'm using* ExtUtils::MakeMaker *to distribute my modules?*

A: There's a little more syntax you'll need to have Apache-Test generate the *t/TEST* file automatically. The following *Makefile.PL* is similar to the *Build.PL* shown in the lab:

```
#!perl

use ExtUtils::MakeMaker;
use Apache::TestMM qw(test clean);
use Apache::TestRun;

Apache::TestMM::filter_args();

Apache::TestRun->generate_script();
```

## CHAPTER 8

Unit Testing
with Test::Class

If you have experience in other object-oriented languages, you may have used unit testing to develop your test cases and test suites. Object-oriented unit testingframeworks are more popular with programming languages such as C# and Java, while the majority of Perl tests are procedural. This isn't to say that one style is better than the other—the choice between styles depends on the goal and structure of your software.

Test::Class is a powerful testing library that allows you to design your tests in the xUnit style. Tests using Test::Class are classes, not just simple test files. This is more complicated to start, but it allows you to organize test cases more easily as well as minimize repetitive testing code, especially for heavily object-oriented projects.

This chapter demonstrates how to write unit testing code in Perl with Test::Class to take advantage of its benefits, including fixtures and inheritance.

Writing Test Cases

Consider a Queue object that stores items to access in first-in, first-out order. Queue allows you to enqueue and dequeue items, returning them in insertion order. You can query a Queue for how many items it contains. Sure, it's simple enough to do this with Perl's basic data structures, but the complexity of Queue could grow quickly as its uses supersede what a normal array provides.

This lab demonstrates how to test Queue by creating a module that subclasses Test::Class.

How do I do that?

Create a directory *Queue/* and save the following as *Queue/Test.pm*:

```perl
package Queue::Test;

use base 'Test::Class';

use Queue;
use Test::More;

sub size : Test(4)
{
    my $q1 = Queue->new();
    isa_ok( $q1, 'Queue' );
    is( $q1->size(), 0, 'an empty queue' );

    my $q2 = Queue->new(qw( howdy bonjour ));
    isa_ok( $q2, 'Queue' );
    is( $q2->size(), 2, 'a queue with some elements' );
}

sub enqueue : Test(2)
{
    my $queue = Queue->new();
    isa_ok( $queue, 'Queue' );

    $queue->enqueue($_) for qw( howdy bonjour );
    is( $queue->size(), 2, 'queue is now larger' );
}

sub dequeue : Test(6)
{
    my $queue = Queue->new();
    isa_ok( $queue, 'Queue' );

    is( $queue->dequeue, undef, 'empty queue' );

    $queue->enqueue($_) for qw( howdy bonjour );
    is( $queue->size(),     2,          'queue is now larger' );
    is( $queue->dequeue(), 'howdy',    'first item'          );
    is( $queue->dequeue(), 'bonjour', 'second item'         );
    is( $queue->size(),     0,          'queue is now smaller' );
}

1;
```

The `Queue` class is fairly simple as far as Perl objects go. Save it as *Queue. pm*:

```perl
package Queue;

use strict;
use warnings;
```

```perl
sub new
{
    my ($class, @items) = @_;
    bless \@items, $class;
}

sub size
{
    my ($self) = @_;
    return scalar @$self;
}

sub enqueue
{
    my ( $self, $item ) = @_;
    push @$self, $item;
}

sub dequeue
{
    my ( $self ) = @_;
    return shift @$self;
}

1;
```

Save the test file as *queue.t*:

```perl
#!perl

use Queue::Test;

Test::Class->runtests();
```

Finally, run *queue.t* with *prove*:

```
$ prove queue.t
queue....#
# Queue::Test->test_dequeue
1..12
ok 1 - The object isa Queue
ok 2 - empty queue
ok 3 - queue is now larger
ok 4 - first item
ok 5 - second item
ok 6 - queue is now smaller
#
# Queue::Test->test_enqueue
ok 7 - The object isa Queue
ok 8 - queue is now larger
#
# Queue::Test->test_size
ok 9 - The object isa Queue
ok 10 - an empty queue
```

```
ok 11 - The object isa Queue
ok 12 - a queue with some elements
ok
All tests successful.
Files=1, Tests=12,  1 wallclock secs ( 0.19 cusr +  0.00 csys =  0.19 CPU)
```

What just happened?

The test file you saved as *queue.t* has a very simple job: to run all of the test methods defined in the Queue::Test class. Test::Class is smart—it keeps track of any module that subclasses it. All you need to do is use your test modules and call runtests() on Test::Class itself.

You can use any Test::Builder testing module with Test::Class, such as Test::Exception or Test::Deep. Most test classes use at least Test::More's basic testing functions.

Subroutine attributes are the things after the subroutine name and before the opening brace. See perldoc attributes to learn more.

To designate a method as containing tests, add a Test(*n*) attribute that declares how many tests the method contains. Test::Class automatically adds them all up and declares a plan for you, so you don't need to scan through giant test files to count all of your is() and ok() functions. If you don't know how many tests a method will contain, use the Test(no_plan) attribute.

If your test methods die or return before the end of the test method, Test::Class will produce fake skipped tests enough times to complete the test count declared in the Test attribute. Dying in a test method produces a test failure, and returning skips the remaining tests in the method. However, if you return when you use Test(no_plan), you won't have any idea if there are tests after the return statement that should have run!

When you run your tests with verbose mode (either by using the -v option with prove or by setting the TEST_VERBOSE environment variable), Test::Class outputs the name of the test method before it runs any tests for that method. This is a nice way to see where certain tests come from while debugging. Also, if you don't specify test descriptions in your test functions, Test::Class uses the name of the current test method as the test description.

What about...

Q: *Should I use* Test *in all of my module names?*

A: The standard naming convention for unit testing is to suffix the class name you're testing with Test. The example code in this lab used this convention for clarity, but naming your classes like this isn't completely necessary.

An alternative naming scheme for the test classes is to name them in the manner of other object-oriented modules. For example, the `Queue::Test::Word` class inherits from `Queue::Test`. Opinions vary on which is the best approach, so choose the style that fits your team and project.

Q: *What if I distribute this module? Will my test classes install along with my other modules?*

A: If your *Makefile.PL* or *Build.PL* doesn't explicitly state what modules it's going to install, yes. By default, `ExtUtils::MakeMaker` and `Module::Build` look in the *lib/* directory of the distribution for any modules to install. If you don't want to install your test classes, see "Using Temporary Databases" in Chapter 6, which describes using a separate *build_lib/* directory for the testing-related modules.

Of course, if your project is a framework you expect people to subclass, installing the test modules will allow them to inherit tests as well

Q: *Can I control the order in which the tests run?*

A: `Test::Class` runs all *groups* of tests in alphabetical order. First, all startup methods run in alphabetical order. Next, the test methods run in alphabetical order. Finally, the shutdown methods run in alphabetical order. For every test method, its setup methods run in alphabetical order. Then the test method itself runs. Finally, its teardown methods run in alphabetical order. ("Creating Test Fixtures," next, explains setup and teardown methods and fixtures.)

Creating Test Fixtures

Imagine writing tests for your car. If you turn the wheel, do the tires turn left? What about right? If you hit the brakes, do the rear lights light up? Of course, before you can perform any of these tests, you need to open the door, sit in the driver's seat, put on the seat belt, and start the car. When you're done, you must stop the car, unbuckle, and disembark. What a pain it would be to perform each step for each individual test—you'd have to get in and start the car three times!

It would be much easier if, before each test, your car arrived fully prepared and then magically transported you to the driver's seat, buckled you in, and fastened your crash helmet securely. This is exactly what fixtures are: parts of an environment created before tests run and removed after the tests finish.

This lab shows how to create fixtures for your tests using setup and tear-down methods, which eliminates duplication and makes your test code more sane.

How do I do that?

Copy the Queue module and *queue.t* test file from "Writing Test Cases." However, the test module needs to change slightly. The new Queue:: Test needs a new method, setup_queues( ), to create a test fixture for the other test methods to use.

Save the following code as *Queue/Test.pm*:

```perl
package Queue::Test;

use base 'Test::Class';

use Queue;
use Test::More;

sub setup_queues : Test( setup => 2 )
{
    my ($self) = @_;

    $self->{empty}    = Queue->new( );
    $self->{twoitems} = Queue->new(qw( howdy bonjour ));

    isa_ok( $self->{$_}, 'Queue' ) for qw( empty twoitems );
}

sub size : Test(2)
{
    my ($self) = @_;
    is( $self->{empty}->size( ),    0, 'an empty queue'                );
    is( $self->{twoitems} >size( ), 2, 'a queue with some elements' );
}

sub enqueue : Test(1)
{
    my ($self) = @_;
    $self->{twoitems}->enqueue($_) for qw( ciao yo );
    is( $self->{twoitems}->size( ), 4, 'queue is now larger' );
}

sub dequeue : Test(3)
{
    my ($self) = @_;

    is( $self->{empty}->dequeue( ),    undef,    'empty queue' );
```

```
    is( $self->{twoitems}->dequeue(), 'howdy',   'first item'  );
    is( $self->{twoitems}->dequeue(), 'bonjour', 'second item' );
}

1;
```

Run *queue.t* verbosely with *prove*:

```
$ prove -v queue.t
queue....#
# Queue::Test->dequeue
1..12
ok 1 - The object isa Queue
ok 2 - empty queue
ok 3 - queue is now larger
ok 4 - first item
ok 5 - second item
ok 6 - queue is now smaller
#
# Queue::Test->enqueue
ok 7 - The object isa Queue
ok 8 - queue is now larger
#
# Queue::Test->size
ok 9 - The object isa Queue
ok 10 - an empty queue
ok 11 - The object isa Queue
ok 12 - a queue with some elements
ok
All tests successful.
Files=1, Tests=12,  0 wallclock secs ( 0.16 cusr +  0.03 csys =  0.19 CPU)
```

What just happened?

Every test method receives a hash reference as its first argument. This is the test object, and it exists to pass data from the fixtures to the tests. Feel free to add whatever you want to it.

Notice the output of prove -v? There are a total of six isa checks, yet setup_queues( ) is the only method that calls isa_ok( ), and it does so only twice. What happened? setup_queues( ) has the attribute Test(setup=> 2).

The setup_queues( ) method prepares and checks the type of two Queue objects that all of the test methods use. Test::Class calls setup_queue( ) before *each* test method, so it runs three times in this test file. Each test method receives two fresh Queue objects in the test object. This simplifies the testing code by eliminating duplicate code, making it easier to add new tests.

Test(setup) is the same as Test(setup => 0). The same goes for the teardown, startup, and shutdown attributes. It never hurts to be verbose, though.

What about...

Q: *What if I need to clean up the fixture after each test?*

A: Use a teardown method by creating a new method with the attribute Test(teardown => *n*). Teardown methods run after each test method.

Q: *Is it possible to have setup and teardown methods for the entire class?*

A: Sure! Test::Class calls these startup and shutdown methods. Declare them with the attributes Test(startup => *n*) and Test(shutdown => *n*), respectively. Each startup and shutdown method runs only once per test file. It receives the test object as the first argument, just like the other test methods.

Because startup methods run only once at the beginning of the test, they do not have the chance to reinitialize whatever they store in the test object as setup methods do.

Inheriting Tests

Your boss thinks highly of your new, shiny Queue module. "Great," she says, "but we need a subclass that will enqueue only single, unhyphenated words." Before you became a confident tester, this might have worried you. It's not scary anymore, though.* Thanks to Test::Class, there's not much more to do.

This lab explains how to write tests for subclasses when you already have Test::Class tests for their parents.

How do I do that?

A subclass inherits from a parent class, so why not have tests inherit from a parent test? Except for the enqueue( ) method, the features of the two classes are the same. Because the tests for Queue enqueue only words, you can reuse the test methods declared in Queue::Test.

Create the directory *Queue/Word/*, and save the following as *Queue/Word/Test.pm*:

```
package Queue::Word::Test;

use base 'Queue::Test';
```

---

* Of course, you might worry if she could see the paper clip trebuchet you've been using to fire paper clips at coworkers.

```
use Queue::Word;
use Test::More;
use Test::Exception;

sub setup_queues : Test( setup => 2 )
{
    my ($self) = @_;

    $self->{empty}    = Queue::Word->new();
    $self->{twoitems} = Queue::Word->new(qw( howdy bonjour ));

    isa_ok( $self->{$_}, 'Queue::Word' ) for qw( empty twoitems );
}

sub check_only_words : Test(5)
{
    my ($self) = @_;

    lives_ok { $self->{empty}->enqueue('wassup') } "can enqueue words";
    lives_ok { $self->{empty}->enqueue('HeLl0') } "case doesn't matter";
    dies_ok  { $self->{empty}->enqueue(1981) } "can't enqueue integers",
    dies_ok  { $self->{empty}->enqueue(10.9) } "can't enqueue decimal";
    dies_ok  { $self->{empty}->enqueue('Transzorp Diode') }
        "can't enqueue names of cyborgs";
}

1;
```

Next, create the Queue::Word module that extends Queue. Save the following code as *Queue/Word.pm*:

```
package Queue::Word;

use strict;
use warnings;

use base 'Queue';

sub enqueue
{
    my ( $self, $item ) = @_;

    die "can only enqueue words, not '$item'"
        unless $item =~ m/ ^ [A-Z]+ $ /ix;

    push @$self, $item;
}

1;
```

Now create a test file, *queue_word.t*, so that it runs the tests for both
classes. Save the following code as *queue_word.t*:

```
#!perl

use Queue::Test;
```

```
use Queue::Word::Test;

Test::Class->runtests();
```

Run it with *prove*:

```
$ prove queue_word.t
queue_word....ok
All tests successful.
Files=1, Tests=31,  1 wallclock secs ( 0.07 cusr +  0.00 csys =  0.07 CPU)
```

What just happened?

Because Queue::Word::Test is a subclass of Queue::Test, it inherits all
the test methods from Queue::Test. It must override setup_queues() so
that the fixture creates objects of the proper class, though.

There's no practical benefit in rewriting the tests for size() and
dequeue(), as the subclass does not change their behavior. The
enqueue() method, however, is more restrictive with its arguments.
check_only_words() tests that the program dies when it receives invalid
arguments.

Calling runtests() tells Test::Class to run all tests in *both* loaded test
classes. Because the test subclass adds additional testing methods, the
queue_word.t test file runs more tests than did the *queue.t* test file.

Skipping Tests with Test::Class

If you need to skip the tests for a class, you might want to skip the tests
for any of its subclasses as well. If you've set up your test class hierarchy
to mimic your real class hierarchy, this is easy to do.

How do I do that?

"Inheriting Tests" showed how to set up tests for the Queue::Word module and its parent class, Queue. Similarly, the test classes for these modules were Queue::Word::Test and Queue::Test, respectively. Suppose
that your project lead won't let you run the tests for Queue::Test and any
of its subclasses after four o'clock because he doesn't believe you'll have
time to fix them before you leave for the day.

Alter *Queue/Test.pm* as follows:

```
package Queue::Test;

use base 'Test::Class';

use Queue;
```

```
use Test::More;

sub SKIP_CLASS
{
    return [ localtime(time) ]->[2] < 16 ? 0 : 'only runs before tea time';
}

sub setup_queues : Test( setup => 2 )
{
    #  ...
}
```

Run *queue.t* with *prove* after four o'clock to see that it skips tests in both
Queue::Test and Queue::Word::Test:

```
$ prove -v queue.t
queue....1..2
ok 1 # skip only runs before tea time
ok 2 # skip only runs before tea time
ok
        2/2 skipped: only runs before tea time
All tests successful, 2 subtests skipped.
Files=1, Tests=2,  0 wallclock secs ( 0.05 cusr +  0.00 csys =  0.05 CPU)
```

What about...

Q: *Can I skip tests for just one particular class?*

A: Sure. Instead of overriding the SKIP_CLASS( ) method, simply call it on
your class and pass it the reason for skipping the tests. Perhaps you
want to to skip the tests for Queue::Test if they run in the morning,
but you don't want to affect its subclasses. Modify *Queue/Test.pm* as
follows:

```
package Queue::Test;

use base 'Test::Class';

use Queue;
use Test::More;

Queue::Test->SKIP_CLASS(
    [ localtime(time) ]->[2] <= 12
    ? 'only runs in the afternoon'
    : 0
);

sub size : Test(4)
{
    #  ...
}
```

Marking Tests as TODO with Test::Class

If you've written the tests for a class but you haven't yet written the implementation, mark the tests as TODO. That way, everyone will know that you expect them to fail. If they succeed, it'll be a nice surprise.

How do I do that?

Test::Class allows you to mark tests in the same manner as tests using Test::More. Simply localize the $TODO variable with the reason why you're putting them off.

Ponder yet again the Queue module and its test module, Queue::Test, from "Writing Test Cases." Imagine that your boss wants you to modify enqueue( ) to refuse to queue undefined values. It's 4:45 p.m. and you want to code the tests so you'll remember your brilliant idea in the morning. Modify *Queue/Test.pm* as follows:

```
sub enqueue : Test(3)
{
    my $queue = Queue->new;
    isa_ok( $queue, 'Queue' );

    $queue->enqueue($_) for qw( howdy bonjour );
    is( $queue->size(), 2, 'queue is now larger' );

    local $TODO = 'decided to disallow undefined items';
    $queue->enqueue(undef);
    is( $queue->size(), 2, "queue size hasn't changed" );
}
```

Run *queue.t* to show that the test fails but has a TODO declaration, just as do the regular TODO tests of Test::More. Now you can go home, confident that you will remember what *Queue.pm* has to do when you return to work in the morning.

What about...

Q: *Can I mark an entire class as TODO?*

A: Unfortunately, Test::Class doesn't provide a simple way to do this. It's probably easier just to skip the tests (see "Skipping Tests with Test::Class," earlier in this chapter).

Testing Everything Else

As pleasant as it might be to believe otherwise, there's a whole world outside of Perl. Fortunately, Perl works well with other programs and other languages, even to the point at which you can use them almost seamlessly from your Perl code.

Good testers don't shy away from testing external code just because it seems difficult. You can use Perl's nice testing libraries and the tricks you've learned so far even if you have to test code written in other languages or programs you can't modify. Perl's that flexible.

This chapter's labs demonstrate how to test Perl programs that you can't refactor into modules, how to test standalone programs, and how to test code that isn't Perl at all.

Writing Testable Programs

Not every useful piece of Perl code fits in its own module. There's a wealth of worthwhile code in scripts and programs. You know the rule: if it's worth using, it's worth testing. How do you test them? Write them to be as testable as possible.

How do I do that?

Imagine that you have a program that applies filters to files given on the command line, sorting and manipulating them before printing them. Save the following file as *filefilter.pl*:

```perl
#!perl

use strict;
use warnings;
```

Simple, well-factored code is easier to test in isolation. Improving the design of your code is just one of the benefits of writing testable code.

```perl
main( @ARGV ) unless caller();

sub main
{
    die "Usage:\n$0 <command> [file_pattern]\n" unless @_;

    my $command     = shift;
    my $command_sub = main->can( "cmd_$command" );
    die "Unknown command '$command'\n" unless $command_sub;

    print join( "\n", $command_sub->( @_ ) );
}

sub sort_by_time
{
    map   { $_->[0] }
    sort  { $a->[1] <=> $b->[1] }
    map   { [ $_, -M $_ ] } @_
}

sub cmd_latest
{
    (sort_by_time( @_ ) )[0];
}

sub cmd_dirs
{
    grep { -d $_ } @_;
}

# return true
1;
```

filefilter.pl ends with "*1;*" so that the *require( )* will succeed. See *perldoc -f require* to learn more.

Testing this properly requires having some test files in the filesystem or mocking Perl's file access operators ("Overriding Built-ins" in Chapter 5). The former is easier. Save the following program as *make_test_files.pl*:

```perl
#!perl

use strict;
use warnings;

use Fatal qw( mkdir open close );
use File::Spec::Functions;

mkdir( 'music_history' ) unless -d 'music_history';

for my $subdir (qw( handel vivaldi telemann ))
{
    my $dir = catdir( 'music_history', $subdir );
    mkdir( $dir ) unless -d $dir;
}

sleep 1;
```

```
    for my $period (qw( baroque classical ))
    {
        open( my $fh, '>', catfile( 'music_history', $period ));
        print $fh '18th century';
        close $fh;
        sleep 1;
    }
```

Save the following test as *test_filefilter.t*:

```
#!perl

use strict;
use warnings;

use Test::More tests => 5;
use Test::Exception;

use File::Spec::Functions;

ok( require( 'filefilter.pl' ), 'loaded file okay' ) or exit;

throws_ok { main() } qr/Usage:/,
    'main() should give a usage error without any arguments';

throws_ok { main( 'bad command' ) } qr/Unknown command 'bad command'/,
    '... or with a bad command given';

my @directories =
(
    'music_history',
    map { catdir( 'music_history', $_ ) } qw( handel vivaldi telemann )
);

my @files = map { catfile( 'music_history', $_ ) } qw( baroque classical );

is_deeply( [ cmd_dirs( @directories, @files ) ], \@directories,
    'dirs command should return only directories' );

is( cmd_latest( @files ), catfile(qw( music_history classical )),
    'latest command should return most recently modified file' );
```

Baroque preceded Classical, of course.

Run make_test_files.pl and then run test_filefilter.t with *prove*:

```
$ prove test_filefilter.t
test_filefilter....ok
All tests successful.
Files=1, Tests=5,  0 wallclock secs ( 0.08 cusr +  0.02 csys =  0.10 CPU
```

What just happened?

The problem with testing Perl programs that expect to run directly from the command line is loading them in the test file without actually running them. The strange first code line of *filefilter.pl* accomplishes this.

The caller() operator returns information about the code that called the currently executing code. When run directly from the command line, there's no caller information, and the program passes its arguments to the main() subroutine. When run from the test script, the program has caller information, so it does nothing.

The rest of the program is straightforward.

The test file requires the presence of some files and directories to test against. Normally, creating test data from within the test itself works, but in this case, part of the filter program relies on Perl's behavior when checking the last modification time of a file. Because Perl reports this time relative to the time at which the test started, it's much easier to create these files before running the test. Normally, this might be part of the build step. Here, it's a separate program: *make_test_files.pl*. The sleep line attempts to ensure that enough time passes between the Baroque and the Classical periods that the filesystem can tell their creation times apart.[*]

The test uses require() to load the program. Test::More::require_ok() is inappropriate here because it expects to load modules, not programs. The rest of the test is straightforward.

What about...

Q: *What if I run this code on a filesystem that can't tell the difference between the modification times of baroque and classical?*

A: That's one purpose of the test. If the test fails, you might need to modify *filefilter.pl* to take that into account. Start by increasing the value of the sleep call in *make_test_files.pl* and see what the limits of your filesystem are.

Q: *What if the program being tested calls* exit() *or does something otherwise scary?*

A: Override it (see "Overriding Built-ins" in Chapter 5).

Q: *When would you do this instead of running filefilter.pl as a separate program (see "Testing Programs," next)?*

A: This technique makes it easier to test the program's internals. Running it as a separate program means that your test has to treat the entire program as a black box. Note that the test here doesn't have to parse

---

* Sure, that's 150 years of musical history, but computers don't have much culture.

Chapter 9: Testing Everything Else

the program's output; it handles the list returned from cmd_dirs( ), and the scalar returned from cmd_latest( ) as normal Perl data structures.

Testing Programs

Perl's a great glue language and there are a lot of other programs in the world worth gluing together—or at least using from your own programs. Maybe your project relies on the behavior of other programs not under your control. That makes them worth testing. Maybe your job *is* testing, and you've realized that Perl and its wealth of testing libraries would be nice to have to test code written in other languages.

Whatever your motivation, Perl is perfectly capable of testing external programs. This lab shows how.

If you have one program on your machine to run all of the examples in this book, it's the Perl executable itself. That makes it a great candidate to test, especially for things you can't really test from within Perl. For example, the Perl core has its own test suite. How does it test Perl's command-line flags that print messages and exit? How does it test whether bad code produces the correct fatal compiler warnings? It runs a fresh Perl instance and examines its output.

See _fresh_perl( ) and _fresh_perl_ is( ) in t/test.pl in the Perl source code.

You can do the same.

How do I do that?

Save the following test file as *perl_exit.t*:

```perl
#!perl

use strict;
use warnings;

use IPC::Run 'run';
use Test::More tests => 7;

my ($out, $err) = runperl( '-v' );
like($out, qr/This is perl/, '-v should print short version message'      );
is(  $err, '',               '... and no error'                           );

($out, $err)    = runperl( '-V' ) ;
like($out, qr/Compiled at/,  '-V should print extended version message'   );
is(  $err, '',               '... and no error'                           );

($out, $err)    = runperl(qw( -e x++ ));
like($err, qr/Can't modify constant.+postincrement/,
                             'constant modification should die with error' );
```

```
        like( $err, qr/Execution.+aborted.+compilation errors/,
                             '... aborting with to compilation errors'   );
        is( $out, '',        '... writing nothing to standard output'    );

        sub runperl
        {
            run( [ $^X, @_ ], \my( $in, $out, $err ) );
            return ($out, $err);
        }
```

*The special
variable $^X
contains the path
to the currently
running Perl
executable. It
comes up often in
testing.*

Run the test file with *prove*:

```
$ prove perl_exit.t
perl_exit....ok
All tests successful.
Files=1, Tests=6,  1 wallclock secs ( 0.28 cusr +  0.05 csys =  0.33 CPU)
```

What just happened?

The IPC::Run module provides a simple and effective cross-platform way to run external programs and collect what they write to standard output and standard error.

The test file defines a subroutine called runperl() to abstract away and encapsulate all of the IPC::Run code. It calls run() with four arguments. The first argument is an array reference of the program to run—here always $^X—and its command-line options. The other arguments are references to three scalar variables to use for the launched program's STDIN, STDOUT, and STDERR handles. runperl() returns only the last two handles, which IPC::Run has helpfully connected to the output of the program.

*None of the tests
yet need to pass
anything to the
launched program,
so returning $in is
useless.*

Each set of tests starts by calling runperl() with the arguments to use when running Perl. The first run performs the equivalent of:

```
$ perl -v

This is perl, v5.8.6 built for powerpc-linux

Copyright 1987-2004, Larry Wall

Perl may be copied only under the terms of either the Artistic License or
the GNU General Public License, which may be found in the Perl 5 source kit.

Complete documentation for Perl, including FAQ lists, should be found on
this system using `man perl' or `perldoc perl'.  If you have access to the
Internet, point your browser at http://www.perl.org/, the Perl Home Page.
```

The tests check to see that the entire message goes out to standard output, with nothing going to standard error.

The second set of tests uses Perl's -V, or verbose, flag to display an even longer version message, which includes information about the compile-time characteristics of Perl as well as the contents of @INC.

Try perl -V yourself. It's a lot of output.

Finally, the last set of tests exercise Perl's handling of an error, specifically leaving the sigil off of a variable. This test is equivalent to the one-liner:

```
$ perl -e "x++"
Can't modify constant item in postincrement (++) at -e line 1, near "x++"
Execution of -e aborted due to compilation errors.
```

All of this output should go to standard error, not standard output. The final test in this set ensures that.

What about...

Q: *Are there any modules that integrate this with* Test::Builder *for me?*

A: Test::Cmd and Test::Cmd::Common have many features, but they also have complex interfaces. They may work best for large or complicated test suites.

Testing Interactive Programs

Unfortunately for testers, lots of useful programs are more than modules, well-factored Perl programs, or shared libraries. They have user interfaces, take input from the keyboard, and even produce output to the screen.

It may seem daunting to figure out how to mock all of the inputs and outputs to test the program. Fortunately, there's a solution. Test::Expect allows you to run external programs, feeding them input and checking their output, all within your test files.

How do I do that?

Think back to your early programming days, when the canonical example of accepting user input was building a calculator. In Perl, you may have written something like *simplecalc.pl*:

```
#!perl

use strict;
use warnings;
```

```perl
    print "> ";

    while (<>)
    {
        chomp;
        last unless $_;

        my ($command, @args) = split( /\s+/, $_ );

        my $sub;
        unless ($sub = __PACKAGE__->can( $command ))
        {
            print "Unknown command '$command'\n> ";
            next;
        }

        $sub->(@args);
        print "> ";
    }

sub add
{
    my $result = 0;

    $result += $_ for @_;
    print join(" + " , @_ ), " = $result\n";
}

sub subtract
{
    my $result = shift;

    print join(" - " , $result, @_ );

    $result -= $_ for @_;
    print " = $result\n";
}
```

Save the file and play with it. Enter the commands add or subtract, followed by multiple numbers. It will perform the appropriate operation and display the results. If you give an invalid command, it will report an error. Enter a blank line to quit.

It's tempting to test this program with the technique shown earlier in "Writing Testable Programs," but the loop is central to the program and difficult to test. Alternately, what if your assignment were to write this code in another language? Fortunately, the same testing technique works for both possibilities.

Save the following test file as *testcalc.t*:

```perl
#!perl

use strict;
```

```
use Test::More tests => 7;
use Test::Expect;

expect_run(
    command => "$^X simplecalc.pl",
    prompt  => '> ',
    quit    => "\n",
);

expect(     'add 1 2 3',      '1 + 2 + 3 = 6', 'adding three numbers'     );
expect_send('subtract 1 2 3',                  'subtract should work'     );
expect_is(  '1 - 2 - 3 = -4',                  '.. producing good results' );
expect_send('weird magic',                     'not dying on bad input'   );
expect_like(qr/Unknown command 'weird/,        '... but giving an error'  );
```

Run it from the directory containing *simplecalc.pl*:

```
$ prove testcalc.t
testcalc....ok
All tests successful.
Files=1, Tests=7,  0 wallclock secs ( 0.27 cusr +  0.02 csys =  0.29 CPU)
```

What just happened?

The test file begins with a call to expect_run( ) to tell Test::Expect about
the program to automate. The command argument provides the command to
launch the program. In this case, it needs to launch *simplecalc.pl* with the
currently executing Perl binary ($^X). The program's prompt is "> ", which
helps the module know when the program awaits input. Finally, the quit
argument contains the sequence to end the program.

The first test calls expect( ), passing the command to send *to* the program and the output expected *from* the program. If those match, the test
passes—actually twice, once for being able to send the data to the program correctly and the second time for the actual results matching the
expected results.

The next test uses expect_send( ) to send data to the program. Though
there's nothing to match, this test passes if the program accepts the input
and returns a prompt.

Now that the program has sent some data, the test can check the results
of the last operation by calling expect_is( ) to match the expected data
directly. It works just like Test::More::is( ), except that it takes the
received data from the program run through Test::Expect, not from an
argument to the function.

The expect_like( ) function is similar. It applies a regular expression to
the data returned from the last operation performed by the program.

Test::Expect works like the Expect automation tool, which also has Perl modules in the form of Expect.pm and Expect::Simple.

What about...

Q: *That's pretty simple, but I need to use more prompts and handle potential errors. What can I do?*

A: Test::Expect uses Expect::Simple internally. The latter module provides more options to drive external programs. You may have to use Test::More::is() and Test::More::like() to perform comparisons, but Expect::Simple handles the messy work of connecting to and driving an external program.

Testing Shared Libraries

You must have the Inline::C module installed and you must have a C compiler available and configured.

Here's a secret: Perl's testing modules aren't just good for testing Perl. They can test anything you can call from Perl. With a little bit of help from a few other modules, it's easy to test shared libraries—compiled C code, for example—as if it were normal Perl code.

How do I do that?

Suppose that you want to test your C math library, *libm*. Specifically, you need to exercise the behavior of the fmax() and fmin() functions, which find the maximum or minimum of two floating point values, respectively. Save the following code as *test_libmath.t*:

```perl
#!perl

BEGIN
{
        chdir 't' if -d 't';
}

use strict;
use warnings;
use Test::More tests => 6;

use Inline C =>
        Config   =>
                 LIBS   => '-lm',
                 ENABLE => 'AUTOWRAP'
;

Inline->import( C => <<END_HEADERS );
        double fmax( double, double );
        double fmin( double, double );
END_HEADERS

is( fmax(  1.0,  2.0 ),  2.0, 'fmax() should find maximum of two values'  );
is( fmax( -1.0,  1.0 ),  1.0, '... and should handle one negative'        );
```

```
is( fmax( -1.0, -7.0 ), -1.0, '... or two negatives'                  );
is( fmin(  9.3,  1.7 ),  1.7, 'fmin() should find minimum of two values' );
is( fmin(  2.0, -1.0 ), -1.0, '... and should handle one negative'    );
is( fmin( -1.0, -6.0 ), -6.0, '... or two negatives'                  );
```

Run the tests with *prove*:

```
$ prove test_math.t
test_math....ok
All tests successful.
Files=1, Tests=6,  0 wallclock secs ( 0.17 cusr +  0.01 csys =  0.18 CPU)
```

What just happened?

The Inline::C module allows easy use of C code from Perl. It's a power-ful *and* simple way to build or to link to C code without writing Perl extension code by hand. The test starts as usual, changing to the *t/* directory and declaring a plan. Then it uses Inline, passing some config-uration data that tells the module to link against the m library (*libm.so* on Unix and Unix-like systems) and generate wrappers for C functions auto-matically.

Inline::C caches compiled code in an __Inline/ directory. The test file changes to t/ to localize the cache in the test subdirectory.

The only C code necessary to make this work occurs in the import( ) call, which passes the function signatures of the C functions to wrap from the math library. When Inline processes this code, it writes and compiles some C code to create the wrappers from these functions, and then makes the wrappers available to the test as the functions fmax( ) and fmin( ).

The rest of the test file tests some of the boundary conditions for these two functions.

What about...

Q: *Does this work with other languages besides C?*

A: There are Inline modules for various languages, including C++, Java, and PHP. The same or similar techniques work there too.

Q: *Can I achieve the same thing by using XS or SWIG to generate bindings?*

A: Absolutely. Inline is very easy for simple and moderate bindings, but it doesn't do anything that you can't do elsewhere.

Q: *Can* Inline *handle passing and returning complex data structures such as C-structs?*

A: Yes. See the Inline::C cookbook from the Inline distribution for examples.

Index

We'd like to hear your suggestions for improving our indexes. Send email to *index@oreilly.com*.

operators
    built-in, overriding, 83–88
    overriding, 106–108

P

package variables, changing for
    tests, 102–106
page_links_ok() function,
    Test::WWW::Mechanize
    module, 135
Perl
    compilation environment for, setting
        up, 3
    history of automated testing for, xiii
    version requirements for, xiv
PERL5LIB variable, using PREFIX
    with, 4
PHP code, testing, 173
Plain Old Documentation (POD)
    format, 61
plan() function
    Apache::Test module, 146
    Test::More module, 22
POD files
    testing coverage of, 63–65
    testing syntax of, 61–63
POD (Plain Old Documentation)
    format, 61
PodMaster, list of ppm repositories, 2
POST() function, Apache::TestRequest
    module, 147
ppm utility, installing test modules
    using, 2
programs
    external, testing, 167–169
    interactive, testing, 169–172
    testing, 163–167
prompt() function
    ExtUtils::MakeMaker module, 70
    Module::Build module, 70, 72
prove program, 6–9
    diagnostic output, 27
    output from failed tests, 18
    running wrong number of tests, 9
PUT() function, Apache::TestRequest
    module, 147

Q

quality (see "kwalitee", validating)

R

re() function, Test::Deep module, 31
regular expressions, creating for
    comparisons, 31
require() function, 166
require_ok() function, Test::More
    module, 14
results of tests
    collecting automatically, 76–79
    interpreting, 7
row_ok() function, Test::DatabaseRow
    module, 115
"Running and Developing Tests with
    the Apache::Test
    Framework", 148
runperl() function, IPC::Run
    module, 168
runtests() function, Test::Class
    module, 154, 160

S

scripts, testing, 163–167
SERVERROOT variable, 143
set_true() method, Test::MockObject
    module, 96
setup attribute, Test::Class
    module, 157
shared libraries, testing, 172–173
shutdown attribute, Test::Class
    module, 158
SIGNATURE file, 66
signature_ok() function, Test::Signature
    module, 67
signatures, distribution, 66–67
SKIP blocks, 21
skip() function, Test::More module, 21
SKIP_CLASS() method, 160
skip_reason() function, Apache::Test
    module, 146
smoketesting, 56–60
startup attribute, Test::Class
    module, 158
statement coverage, 44

tests (*continued*)
  results of
    collecting automatically, 76–79
    interpreting, 7
  running, 5–7
    arbitrary number of, 11
    individually, 6
    manually, 6
    on installation, 73–76
    on installation, user
      deciding, 69–73
    wrong number of, 9
  separate files for, 40
  skipping all tests, 22–23
  skipping specific tests, 19–21
  writing, 10–12
Test::Signature module, 66, 67
Test::Simple module, 10–12
test_test() function,
      Test::Builder::Tester
      module, 52
TEST_VERBOSE argument, make test
      program, 7
TEST_VERBOSE variable, 154
Test::Warn module, 34
Test::WWW::Mechanize module, 133,
      134
throws_ok() function, Test::Exception
      module, 38
tie() function, Test::Output::Tie
      module, 106
title_is() function,
      Test::WWW::Mechanize
      module, 134
title_like() function,
      Test::WWW::Mechanize
      module, 134
title_unlike() function,
      Test::WWW::Mechanize
      module, 134
TODO blocks, 23–25, 162
typographical conventions used in this
      book, xv

U

unit testing, 151
unlike() function, Test::More
      module, 18
UPLOAD() function,
      Apache::TestRequest
      module, 147

use_ok() function, Test::More
      module, 13, 14
user, deciding which tests to run on
      installation, 69–73

V

–v (verbose) option, prove
      command, 6, 12, 17, 154
variables
  defined in modules, required for
      test, 14
  package variables, changing for
      tests, 102–106
version requirements for Perl, xiv

W

warning_is() function, Test::Warn
      module, 35
warning_like() function, Test::Warn
      module, 35
warnings, testing, 34–36
warnings_are() function, Test::Warn
      module, 35
web site resources
  CPAN, 3
  CPAN downloads, 39
  CPAN Testers, 73
  CPANTS (CPAN Testing Service), 79
  for this book, xvii
  GnuPG, 66
  PodMaster, list of ppm
      repositories, 2
  Test::Harness module, 5
  Test::MockDBI module, information
      about, 125
web sites, testing
  backend database
      features, 127–132
  frontend features, 132–135
  HTML validity, 138–140
  recording and playing back
      browsing sessions, 135–138
write_message() function, testing, 105

X

$^X variable, 87, 168

Y

y_n() method, Module::Build
      module, 72

About the Authors

Ian Langworth (*http://langworth.com/*) has been writing Perl for years and actively involved in the community since 2003. He has contributed a handful of modules to the CPAN, most of which are Kwiki related. He has spoken at Perl-related conferences such as LISA and YAPC. Ian is also the author of the surprisingly widespread utility Cadubi, which is packaged with many free operating systems.

Ian is currently studying computer science and cognitive psychology at Northeastern University. While pursuing a degree, he's participating in a volunteer systems administration group and working toward making robust and high-qualuty code an easier goal to achieve.

He currently resides in Boston, Massachusetts, where he participates in the local Boston Perl Mongers group and lives precariously close to Fenway Park.

chromatic is the technical editor of the O'Reilly Network, covering open source, Linux, development, and Perl. He's the author of the *Extreme Programming Pocket Guide* and *Running Weblogs with Slash*, and the editor of *BSD Hacks* and *Gaming Hacks*. chromatic is the original author of Test::Builder, the foundation for most modern testing modules in Perl 5, and has written a number of tests for core Perl. He's given testing tutorials and presentations at several Perl conferences, including OSCON, and written several articles on testing for Perl.com. He lives just west of Portland, Oregon, with two cats, a creek in his backyard, and, as you may have guessed, several unfinished projects.

Colophon

Our look is the result of reader comments, our own experimentation, and feedback from distribution channels. Distinctive covers complement our distinctive approach to technical topics, breathing personality and life into potentially dry subjects.

The *Developer's Notebook* series is modeled on the tradition of laboratory notebooks. Laboratory notebooks are an invaluable tool for researchers and their successors.

The purpose of a laboratory notebook is to facilitate the recording of data and conclusions as the work is being conducted, creating a faithful and immediate history. The notebook begins with a title page that includes the owner's name and the subject of research. The pages of the notebook should be numbered and prefaced with a table of contents. Entries must be clear, easy to read, and accurately dated; they should use simple, direct language to indicate the name of the experiment and the steps taken. Calculations are written out carefully and relevant thoughts and ideas recorded. Each experiment is introduced and summarized as it is added to the notebook. The goal is to produce comprehensive, clearly organized notes that can be used as a reference. Careful documentation creates a valuable record and provides a practical guide for future developers.

Adam Witwer was the production editor and Norma Emory was the copyeditor for *Perl Testing: A Developer's Notebook*. Ann Schirmer proofread the text. Matt Hutchinson and Darren Kelly provided quality control. Angela Howard wrote the index.

Edie Freedman designed the cover of this book. Karen Montgomery produced the cover layout with InDesign CS using the Officina Sans and JuniorHandwriting fonts.

David Futato designed the interior layout. This book was converted by Keith Fahlgren to FrameMaker 5.5.6 with a format conversion tool created by Erik Ray, Jason McIntosh, Neil Walls, and Mike Sierra that uses Perl and XML technologies. The text font is Adobe Boton; the heading font is ITC Officina Sans; the code font is LucasFont's TheSans Mono Condensed; and the handwriting font is a modified version of JuniorHandwriting made by Tepid Monkey Foundry, and modified by O'Reilly. The illustrations that appear in the book were produced by Robert Romano, Jessamyn Read, and Lesley Borash using Macromedia FreeHand 9 and Adobe Photoshop 6. This colophon was written by Colleen Gorman.

Better than e-books

Buy *Perl Testing: A Developer's Notebook* and access
the digital edition FREE on Safari for 45 days.

Go to www.oreilly.com/go/safarienabled
and type in coupon code Y2RB-VF3Q-ECCN-6WQM-I7EE

Search
over 2000 top
tech books

Download
whole chapters

Cut and Paste
code examples

Find
answers fast

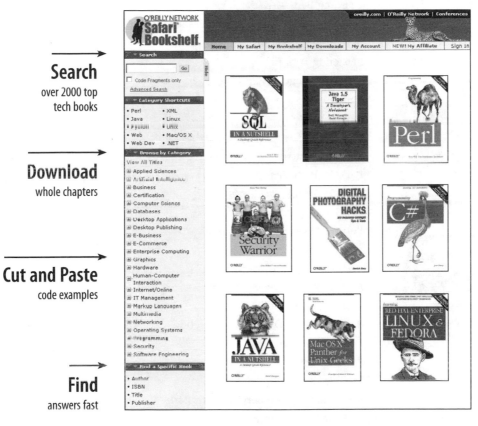

Search Safari! The premier electronic reference
library for programmers and IT professionals

Related Titles from O'Reilly

Perl

Advanced Perl Programming, *2nd Edition*

CGI Programming with Perl, *2nd Edition*

Computer Science & Perl Programming: The Best of the Perl Journal

Embedding Perl in HTML with Mason

Games, Diversions, & Perl Culture: The Best of the Perl Journal

Learning Perl, *4th Edition*

Learning Perl Objects, References and Modules

Mastering Algorithms with Perl

Mastering Perl/Tk

Mastering Regular Expressions, *2nd Edition*

Perl & LWP

Perl & XML

Perl 6 and Parrot Essentials, *2nd Edition*

Perl Best Practices

Perl CD Bookshelf, *Version 4.0*

Perl Cookbook, *2nd Edition*

Perl Debugger Pocket Reference

Perl for System Administration

Perl Graphics Programming

Perl in a Nutshell, *2nd Edition*

Perl Pocket Reference, *4th Edition*

Perl Template Toolkit

Perl Testing: A Developer's Notebook

Practical mod_perl

Programming the Perl DBI

Programming Perl, *3rd Edition*

Programming Web Services with Perl

Regular Expression Pocket Guide

RT Essentials

Web, Graphics & Perl/Tk: The Best of the Perl Journal

XML Publishing with AxKit

Keep in touch with O'Reilly

Download examples from our books

To find example files from a book, go to:
www.oreilly.com/catalog select the book,
and follow the "Examples" link.

Register your O'Reilly books

Register your book at *register.oreilly.com*
Why register your books? Once you've
registered your O'Reilly books you can:

- Win O'Reilly books, T-shirts or discount
  coupons in our monthly drawing.

- Get special offers available only to
  registered O'Reilly customers.

- Get catalogs announcing new books
  (US and UK only).

- Get email notification of new editions
  of the O'Reilly books you own.

Join our email lists

Sign up to get topic-specific email announ-
cements of new books and conferences,
special offers, and O'Reilly Network
technology newsletters at:

elists.oreilly.com

It's easy to customize your free elists subscription so you'll get exactly the O'Reilly news
you want.

Get the latest news, tips, and tools

www.oreilly.com

- "Top 100 Sites on the Web"—PC Magazine
- CIO Magazine's Web Business 50 Awards

Our web site contains a library of comprehensive product information (including book
excerpts and tables of contents), downloadable
software, background articles, interviews with
technology leaders, links to relevant sites, book
cover art, and more.

Work for O'Reilly

Check out our web site for current
employment opportunities:

jobs.oreilly.com

Contact us

O'Reilly Media, Inc.
1005 Gravenstein Hwy North
Sebastopol, CA 95472 USA
Tel: 707-827-7000 or 800-998-9938
　　(6am to 5pm PST)
Fax: 707-829-0104

Contact us by email

For answers to problems regarding
your order or our products:
order@oreilly.com

To request a copy of our latest catalog:
catalog@oreilly.com

For book content technical questions
or corrections: **booktech@oreilly.com**

For educational, library, government,
and corporate sales: **corporate@oreilly.com**

To submit new book proposals to our
editors and product managers:
proposals@oreilly.com

For information about our international
distributors or translation queries:
international@oreilly.com

For information about academic
use of O'Reilly books:
adoption@oreilly.com
or visit:
academic.oreilly.com

For a list of our distributors outside
of North America check out:
international.oreilly.com/distributors.html

Order a book online

www.oreilly.com/order_new

Our books are available at most retail and online bookstores.
To order direct: 1-800-998-9938 • *order@oreilly.com* • *www.oreilly.com*
Online editions of most O'Reilly titles are available by subscription at *safari.oreilly.com*